Free Range Faith

How to Express Your Faith Without Selling Your Soul

Glenn Hager

COMMUNITAS BOOKS
Free Range Faith: How Express Your Faith Without Selling Your Soul
Glenn Hager

General Editor: Rachel Sagar
Cover Design: Robert Crum

ISBN-13: 9780692628911
ISBN-10: 0692628916
Library of Congress Control Number: 2014903432
CreateSpace Independent Publishing Platform
North Charleston, South Carolina

Published in the United States by Communitas Books.

Version 1.1
Printed by CreateSpace, a DBA of the On-Demand Publishing, LLC

Acknowledgements

Bob Crum did a brilliant job on the cover. That farm boy background served you (and me) well.

Rachel Sagar very quickly picked up editing duties and somehow met my timeline. Here is yet another successful partnership between the United Sates and the United Kingdom.

Patty Hager has put up with me for forty-one years, including allowing me to pursue this madness called writing. She deserves a trophy.

Boyd, the cute and cuddly longhaired Chihuahua, has been my faithful writing companion, even though he is usually asleep on the couch and completely covered by a throw blanket. He has been a good listener and very affirming.

To my children, Michelle and Nathan, their
marriage partners, and their children

I sincerely hope that you and all of those who read
these pages will embrace a faith in Christ that is
real, vibrant, and meaningful. Institutions and
traditions may have failed you, but he never will.

Contents

Contents

Introduction

The American church is in crisis mode.

- Of the 250,000 Protestant churches in America, 200,000 are either stagnant (with no growth) or declining. That is 80% of the churches in America and maybe the one you attend, if you attend at all.
- 4,000 churches close their doors every single year.
- There is less than half of the number of churches today than there were only 100 years ago.
- Since 1950, there are 1/3rd fewer churches in the U.S.
- 3,500 people leave the church every single day.[1]
- Despite what people SAY about weekly attendance, the true weekly (attendance) rate is closer to 25%.
- The percent who say they "never" attend church has risen steadily over the last 30 years as people shift from infrequent attendance to non-attendance.[2]
- Churchgoing is slowly but incontrovertibly losing its role as a normative part of American life. In the 1990s, roughly one out of every seven unchurched adults had never experienced regular church attendance. Today, that percentage has increased to nearly one-quarter. Buried within these numbers are at least two important conclusions: 1) Church is becoming increasingly unfamiliar to millions of Americans, and yet 2) the

churchless are still largely comprised of de-churched adults.

- When the unchurched were asked to describe what they believe are the positive and negative contributions of Christianity in America, almost half (49%) could not identify a single favorable impact of the Christian community.[3]

I am part of the institutional church's crisis because I left it after three decades of support, including two decades as a pastor.

Now, I am trying to figure out how to simply live life loving God and loving people. It sounds deceptively simple, but its simplicity is wrapped in the complexity of what I have been taught all my life.

That teaching led me to pray more, and to try harder. But in the end, I only felt more guilty and shame-filled. I have been a responsible leader and supporter of the church, studied the Bible in great detail, and availed myself to the latest and greatest teaching for over three decades, but that stuff didn't really work for me either. I know there is something more, something different. I believe there is a more real way to experience and express my faith.

In recent years, I have been untangling myself from much of what I was taught, and from what I have taught others. My goal is a faith expression that is rooted in the ways of Jesus and that works in everyday life. I join countless others in being one of the lab rats in this great experiment. We are searching for something other than traditional approaches to Christianity that separate our existence into categories of religious and secular and enshrouds faith with forms and structures that don't remind us much of Jesus.

Free Range Faith closely follows my previous book, *An Irreligious Faith*. In the first book, I laid the foundation for this one as I told the story of my transformation from dyed-in-the-wool church insider to disillusioned outsider. I explored the counter-intuitive ways of Jesus and how the church could resemble him a bit more. Lastly, I focused on validating those who had transitioned out of the church and were forging a new faith that was not dependent upon an institution. That is exactly where I want to pick up with this book.

I can think of a lot of people who would say something like, "Glenn, are you nuts? You can't turn your back upon 2,000 years of teaching and tradition. Yours is an experiment of sour grapes. You got burned by the church and let it turn you into a cranky old guy who slams it every chance you get."

But then, I can think of a lot of other people, who would say something like; "Institutional Christianity has been so unlike Jesus for so long that most of my friends consider it totally irrelevant. The only way to follow Jesus is apart from the institutional church."

My conclusion is that different people are at different places on their journey, and there is no need to vilify anyone. However, the facts point to a continually growing movement of people with an irreligious faith who are turning away from the institution and hungering for more authentic and integrated ways to express their spirituality.

The first section of this book is a study in contrasts, the old ways versus the new ways. It's tricky because the new ways aren't really new, but they do stand in contrast to so much of what we consider to be contemporary Christianity.

Rather than pit the two approaches against each other, I am simply trying to describe a way forward for people who have turned their backs on the old, institutional-bound expressions of faith. These "new" ways attempt to get to the very core of what it means to live life, loving Jesus, and others, in an authentic manner that is totally integrated into what we do and who we are. I am attempting to separate following Jesus from institutional practices and to couple the ways of Jesus to our day-to-day lives.

The second section of this book will take us into some lessons that I and other fellow travelers have embraced in our transition from institutionalists to independent-minded people of faith.

Trying to figure how to live life with a sense of meaning and purpose is a journey that takes a lifetime. Trying to discern what is core truth and what has, through the centuries, encased that truth like a layer of corrosion on an ancient piece of metal is a tricky assignment. But that is my mission. I am still trying to unpackage what it means to love Jesus and love others. I am looking for the simple, the practical, and the beautiful. I have to do it for myself, and for all the others who are on this journey.

Transitions:

Finding "New" Ways to Express Your Faith

People who have left (or ignore) the institutional church need to find new avenues of spiritual expression and that can be rather challenging when you are used to having everything dictated to you.

Those who have little experience with, or use for the church would do well to peer closer to see the clear difference between the brilliant ideal and its tainted institutional expression. Then, hopefully, they will distinguish the core truth from the way it has been expressed.

So, in this section, I take us on a walk through the Christian Hall of Fame of those timeworn practices like the worship service, the offering, Bible study, prayer, and missions work. With each of these I will attempt to chisel away the centuries of corrosion to see if there is something valuable at the core. Not everything that has built up over the centuries of Christian tradition is corrosive to that core but, unfortunately, much of it is. Lastly, I will try to discern practical ways to implement that core truth into real life today.

I fear that I might come off as a bit pope-ish, pontificating about how one should practice his faith, setting myself up as judge of time-honored traditions. But I am also concerned that my mere mention of those ancient practices may lead some people to think this is just another book telling them how they ought to live the "Christian life." It is not.

Actually, I am being autobiographical in relating my personal experience, first from within the institutional church and then, as an outsider. My sincere hope is that my story overlaps with your story.

one

Finally Feeling Alive

Exhausting Sabbaths

The more traditional church schedules seem to have been designed to exhaust people on what is supposed to be their appointed day of rest. Sunday church schedules used to include Sunday School, followed by a church service, followed by another church service in the evening. Those involved in leadership roles would often find themselves at committee and board meetings also squeezed into their "day of rest."

For pastors, it is even worse. Since I was a pastor for over twenty years, I know what it is like to get up hours before my church members on a day when most people are sleeping in. There was so much on my shoulders. I had to review the sermon to see if I had it more or less memorized, so I could have a natural, spontaneous-seeming delivery. Some busy weeks caused me to put off way too much of the preparation process until the last minute. On those Sunday mornings I was in panic mode and had to get up even earlier. I also had to make sure everyone on the platform knew their role in the service. I prayed with them and tried to keep them calm and encouraged as we all approached the hour of our public presentation, not unlike actors performing in a live theater production.

Since I pastored both a new church and a church that had sold its building and restarted in rented facilities, I was also involved in setting up. There was all of the stuff for the nursery and the children's area that had to be put in place as we tried to make a theater or school look like a well-appointed and comfortable environment for kids. In the latter years, there were tons of tech gear, guitars, keyboards, amps, drum sets, mics, a soundboard, lots of cables, computers, projection equipment, and large speakers to be temporarily installed in rented quarters. I was usually sweaty before the service even began.

Preaching was one of my greatest joys and biggest stresses. I love creative communication and connecting with people, but being "God's spokesman" was a weighty task. I had to interpret the text right, communicate it with power and conviction, hold people's attention, and move them to a desired goal (repentance, hopefulness, a sense of personal responsibility, taking a next step, etc.).

I also had to be available to everyone before and after the service and was always the last person out of the building on Sunday. By lunch, I could hardly finish the meal and remain conscious.

Such is the charmed life of the pastor.

For the average church member, Sundays are much less exhausting but still very strenuous. You have to get up early on a day when your natural biological rhythm tells you to sleep in. Then you dress nicely and put on your happy face, regardless of how you really feel. Eventually, you go sit with other people who have also dragged themselves out of bed and put on their happy faces. As the service begins, you hold out a faint hope for inspiration, or at least, consciousness, through the presentation and the sermon. Of course, you have already threatened (or bribed) your children in the hope of them not embarrassing you.

Family preparation for the Sunday morning service qualifies as comedy (or tragedy) depending on your frame of mind at the time. As a parent, you have the responsibility of not only preparing yourself for the momentous occasion, but each of your children as well. On the day when you would dearly love to take a break from your morning routine, you once again have the duty of badgering obstinate people from their slumber. From there, you herd them through your limited bathroom facilities, make sure they are suitably attired, so as not to create a bad impression of your parenting skills, feed them a pop tart or something that takes no more than five minutes to prepare and consume, and then, strap them in the car.

Usually something spills at the last minute or someone can only find one shoe. Your day of rest is already a day of stress. Invariably, at least one person in the family is in a bad mood, which infects the others at a rate that would alarm the National Center for Disease Control. But after vicious threats and raised voices, you pull into the parking lot and blackmail the little human beings into feigning acceptable public behavior and manners.

Such a joyous family occasion. Patty and I did it for years. I am sure our kids could tell some stories.

The Sabbath Principle

The word, "Sabbath" may stir up mental images of stern looking, old-fashioned, religious people who are strict and rigid in their ways. Or you may call to mind the blue laws that used to prohibit commerce on Sundays, resulting in most stores being closed one day a week.

But the Sabbath is simply a weekly day set apart for rest and worship.

Genesis records that God began the Sabbath principle by resting on the seventh day of creation and declaring it holy (Genesis 2:3-4). It was formalized in the Ten Commandments and work was forbidden on the Sabbath (Exodus 20:8-11). The Sabbath was also declared to be a sign of the covenant between God and his people, the Israelites (Exodus 31:13-17), and was regarded as a reminder of their deliverance from Egyptian bondage (Deuteronomy 5:12-15). Observed from sundown Friday to sundown Saturday, the penalty for violating Sabbath regulations was banishment, or death (Exodus 31:14).

The Israelites were also instructed to observe special Sabbaths that coincided with annual festivals, the Day of Atonement being one (Leviticus 23:32). There was even a sabbatical year observed in which the ground was allowed to rest and the fields remained untilled and unharvested to the benefit of the poor and the "beasts of the field" (Exodus 23:10-11). Interestingly, the regulations on the Sabbath year also granted freedom to slaves and the relaxation of debts (Exodus 21: 2-6, Deuteronomy 15: 1-6), similar to The Year of Jubilee.

The Old Testament teaching was exact. Keep the Sabbath because God declared it holy and a day of rest. Let the land rest every seventh year for the benefit of the poor and the animals. Forgive the debts you hold against people. Remember how God brought you out of Egypt.

To keep the Sabbath as outlined in the Old Testament took discipline and preparation. Taking time off of work in a subsistence economy was an act of faith in God's provision. Keeping the Sabbath is at odds with human nature. We put things off to the last minute, like to feel self-sufficient, and want to get all we can.

Since the Puritans, most Christians (English-speaking Protestants, Roman Catholics, and Eastern Orthodox) have equated The Lord's Day (Sunday) with the Sabbath (Friday evening to Saturday evening) as a commemoration of Christ's resurrection, which took place on Sunday. Most other religions also have holy days and declared times for rest and reflection.

Jesus and his disciples repeatedly violated Sabbath regulations. His disciples picked grain on the Sabbath (Matthew 12:1-2) and he healed a man on the Sabbath (Matthew 12: 9-11; Like 13:10-17; Luke 14:1-6). He claimed himself to be the Lord of the Sabbath, saying he desired mercy over sacrifice (Matthew 9:13). He declared, "The Sabbath was made for man, not man for the Sabbath." (Mark 2:27)

Jesus changed everything. He broke the shackles of extreme Sabbath requirements and put it in perspective. He didn't say, "Forget about the Sabbath. It was a bad idea." However, we do find him saying and illustrating that it is more important for someone to keep from starving than worry about fulfilling a religious regulation. It is more important to respond to human need than to feel super pious. Human beings are more important than religious regulations.

He opposed extreme, meticulous, and hurtful insensitivity in keeping the Sabbath, but we don't find him denying the validity of setting aside a day of the week for rest and reflection.

The concept of the five-day workweek and the weekend is a relatively recent idea, born when labor unions in America attempted to accommodate the Jewish Sabbath in a New England cotton mill. Henry Ford adopted the structure in 1926. It spread rapidly through Europe and has very recently been adopted in China. So now much of the world has two days off every week.

The Sabbath principle is simply taking one day a week for rest and reflection, but how does that work in modern life?

A New Sabbath

It is infinitely important to have a good editor. She has the same kind of power as a record producer who takes a good song and turns it into a great record (MP3) that is a beautiful piece of artistic expression that touches people on an emotional level.

In my last book, *An Irreligious Faith,* my editor, Erin, put a note in the sidebar of the manuscript that generated one of those beautiful "Ah ha!" moments in my mind. I had written about how I was enjoying a more refreshing Sabbath by not going to church, than when I was going to church. In particular, I mentioned how during football season, my wife and I would gather at my son and daughter-in-law's to watch the Kansas City Chiefs as part of the Chief's Kingdom diaspora in the Chicago area. Often, there would be other family members and friends there. Always, there was amazing food to share. Erin's note in the sidebar: "Maybe, that was church."

I used to think very poorly of people who were like the kind of person I had become. I didn't understand, appreciate, or respect those people who rushed home from church or skipped it all together because of a stupid game. I regarded it as a sad case of misplaced priorities. They should have known that the church is the most important thing in the world and their religious-like fervor over a stupid game was some sort of pagan flip flop of values. Then, I became one of "them."

As I mentioned, my Sundays as a pastor were exhausting, involving a huge expenditure of physical, mental, and emotional energy. Back in the day, we also had an evening service on Sunday, so I had to recuperate from the first service and re-energize for the second one (with a new sermon) in only a few short hours.

My favorite time of the day was when it was all over, when I didn't need to say something profound. I didn't need to move people with an eloquently worded prayer and I didn't need to listen to their problems. I loved going out to the frozen yogurt shop with friends and just relaxing after I had made that final public performance. Even better, was coming home and having a late dinner of tomato soup and grilled cheese sandwiches (a family tradition) and watching TV.

There was one thing that kept me going during those years; I felt that what I was doing was filled with meaning and purpose. But that feeling began to change when I became a spectator and was no longer an actor on stage. Then I experienced what most people experience on a Sunday. I would go to church expecting inspiration, enjoy it, or endure it, do a postgame analysis on the way home in the car with my wife, and then get on with the day.

A lot of the church services I attended after being a pastor were pretty good. Some were mediocre. But something changed in me. I became discontent being a spectator. I was looking for the church to take it to the next level, to make it real, to take some risks to move toward greater authenticity, but I never found an appetite for that among the stay-the-course church leadership.

So, I became more and more frustrated until it became burdensome for me to attend a Sunday church service. Maybe, it was something in the service that set me off, or how I was treated when I offered a suggestion, or knowing that the church wasn't open to change. Instead of being encouraged, I would leave church frustrated.

For me, church as I had known it was no longer working. Sunday was no longer a special day, except in that it was more frustrating than other days of the week. For me, attending a church service had become a total disconnect with the Sabbath principle. It was not restful, refreshing, or reflective. I had to find a new way to enjoy a Sabbath.

For most of my life I have been obsessed with trying to get things right. I have been hypersensitive to the teachings of Evangelicalism which constantly nagged me about what a good

Christian does and does not do. That list is a web of expectations nearly as involved as those of the legalists of Jesus' day, and turned being a child of God into attempting to follow a judicial code (and failing). I have been persistently striving to comply with those expectations, and berating myself when I failed to do so.

But that has been changing the last few years as I have granted myself permission to enjoy life and do things simply because I like doing them and because they refresh me.

After all, Jesus went to parties, accepted lots of invitations to social events, played with children, and told some great stories. He said he came so we could enjoy the fullness of life. Howard Thurman put it like this, "Don't ask yourself what the world needs. Ask yourself what makes you come alive and then go do that. Because what the world needs is people who have come alive." Taking note of the subtitle of my first book, I need to feed life and starve religion. I had that backwards for far too many years; by feeding religion, I was starving life.

Jesus said the Sabbath, a time of rest, reflection, and refreshment, "was made for man, not man for the Sabbath" (Mark 2:27). Obviously, the Sabbath principle is important, not just for spiritual reasons, but for our mental and emotional health as well. There is no better time to do those things that breathe life into your soul than your personal celebration of the Sabbath. It doesn't have to be any particular day of the week, but Sunday is probably the best day of the week for a lot of people's schedules.

What breathes life into your soul? What refreshes you? What do you enjoy? What sets your mind at peace? What renews your energy? What helps you to regain your equilibrium? What makes you feel alive? Make a list. You had better take a few moments to do it now or you never will. It's that important.

Begin doing those things regularly. Make it as important as anything else on your schedule, because it may be the most important thing on your schedule since it energizes you to do the rest of the things you need to do.

I came to realize that if I couldn't take care of myself, I couldn't help anyone else. Soul care is perhaps our primary responsibility and renewing ourselves is as holy as serving a homeless person. Our personal wellbeing and our ability to contribute to the wellbeing of others are wired together. There is a unique energy that flows in both directions.

I have repeatedly fallen into two traps and sometimes I still do, though not as often. I would ruminate over the past, my failures and my wounds; a backdoor strategy for depression and inertia. The other trap was that, out of an overgrown sense of personal responsibility, I would work so hard for so long without coming up for air that eventually I would simply crash. Both ways, I ignored caring for my own soul.

For me the core of soul care means two things, remembering who I am in God's eyes and being in touch with myself enough to know what makes me feel alive.

The traditional message of Evangelicalism goes something like this. "You're a no good sinner, rotten to the core, bound for Hell, and your only hope is to accept Jesus' payment for your sin and start improving the way you live." (I got kind of depressed just from writing those words.) I won't quibble with the propensity of humans toward sin, the reality of a life beyond this one, or the redemptive nature of Christ, but I do take exception to the totally imbalanced perspective of this statement.

For we are also precious in the sight of God, the very pinnacle of his creation, possessing his image and likeness, and uniquely gifted to fulfill an important role in his kingdom, here and now. We could not possibly be more loved, more forgiven, more accepted, or more blessed than we are right now, because God has simply maxed out on all of those things and he doesn't change, no matter what.

To say it is one thing; to believe it is another and to feel it is something different again. People do things that cause me to doubt what God has said about me and has done for me, but my biggest enemy is myself.

Understanding who you really are is the foundation of soul care, being refreshed, and enjoying a Sabbath. Understanding what makes you feel alive, giving yourself permission to do those things, and keeping them in your life is the other part of the foundation.

When I complete a long bike ride along the lakefront of Lake Michigan, I feel like I have done something good. When I wail away playing rhythm guitar to some rock song, I feel a sense of release and refreshment. When I write as honestly as I can about something that is important or fascinating to me, I feel I have created something. When I use my gifts to reach out to people marginalized by the church or culture, then I am rewarded by knowing my life is in alignment with who I really am and who God is. When I laugh with my friends and make them laugh, I am alive. When I am listening to loud, live music and singing and dancing with no fear of embarrassment, I really don't care about anything else. When someone needs me and I do the right thing, I am drawn far away from my self-centered preoccupations. In short these things make me feel alive.

When I neglect them, I get into trouble. I get bored, or want to escape, or I somehow lose my perspective.

The core of human joy and meaning is found in resting, refreshing, relating, creating, and helping. Please, take care of yourself. Be intentional about enjoying the Sabbath principle in your life.

two

Finding God...Everywhere

When Worship Rocks

When I would visit my Black Pentecostal pastor friend's church, I would leave feeling like I had been put through an emotional ringer. It was draining, but cathartic. They had emotionally intense music, singing, swaying, praying, and dancing. There were times of reflection and prayer far more intense than any therapy session I can imagine. It reminded me of when I eat really spicy Mexican food. My face turns red and sweat begins running down my forehead, but I keep eating it because it is so good. When I left a church service there, I would literally be perspiring, but it was good!

Our church band rocked too. There was one very elderly, almost blind lady that would dance down the aisle every Sunday as she was being seated. We got to where we raised hands and swayed. It was a big deal for us to get past our stodgy fundamentalist roots to feel this new freedom of expression.

As a preacher, I felt it was invaluable for the congregation to be "prepared" for the sermon. They needed to be focused, in the mood, roused by praise, and then subdued by worship and reflection.

I immediately found out that people either loved or hated this type of worship. Older, stately people usually hated it and called it worldly, shallow, and inappropriate. Most people loved it. It made them feel alive, in touch with God, and happy they went to a "cool" church.

I have a young adult acquaintance that generally dislikes most anything Christian, but loves U2 and has been to several of their concerts. One time he said to me that a U2 concert was his church.

A great worship service and a great concert are close cousins. What do they have in common?

Intensity. Music has the power to touch us emotionally in a way that brings powerful images to our minds and cuts straight through our personal and intellectual firewalls to reach our heart.

Unity. A worship service is filled with people who love God and a U2 concert is filled with people who love U2. There is a unique, combined intensity, energy, and community when you get a few hundred or a few thousand people together, enthusiastically singing the same song.

Anonymity. A large gathering and a loud band give even us questionable singers permission to sing our hearts out, because no one will hear us.

Elation. It is such a joy to be in a great worship service or a concert of a band you love. While you are singing, you aren't thinking of anything other than the song. You are completely in the moment, overloaded with the sensory stimuli. That's why people pay big bucks for concert tickets.

In the world of modern Evangelicalism, the rousing concert and its accompanying emotional responses have all been given spiritual terminology and equated with worship. That's why worship happens once a week for so many people. After all, it takes a talented band and a large group of people. Maybe there was some sincere worship that took place there, but one thing is for sure, it was a good concert.

Yet it seems weird to confine ascribing worth to God to a brief weekly, corporate activity that is apart from the regular course of life.

For many years, I approached my faith from a fundamentalist perspective that placed a lot of emphasis on being right. The downside to that perspective is the latent sense of arrogance and exclusivity that holds that everyone who believes a little differently is wrong. Every church thinks they do things the right way and that a lot of other churches do things the wrong way. That extends to the way they do corporate worship.

Some churches have emotionally driven worship services, like I described earlier. Some stress theological correctness, placing the emphasis on imparting biblical knowledge. Some just sort of go through the motions of whatever their ritual happens to be. So, on Sunday morning, depending on where you attend, you may be deeply moved, intellectually affirmed, or simply satisfied that you did your duty and showed up. Now you can get on with life.

Theologically laced hymns written in the nineteen century or earlier, accompanied by scripture readings and a lengthy sermon full of contextual nuances that leaves you feeling smarter and even more correct in your beliefs, is the fare in some houses of worship.

Good old-fashioned hymn singin' and good old time preachin', punctuated by a few "amens" is served up in the congregation of another church.

Processions, priests, sacraments, vestments, and homilies within the confines of beautiful architecture are the trappings for the more formal of worshippers who prefer symbolism, anchored in church history as an expression of their faith.

All of it is passed off as worship or as a worship service. I get how these things can connect with some people, but it seems kind of contrived and very limiting to me. It is a presentation, designed with a desired response in mind.

The idea of an omnipotent, omniscient, omnipresent God being the center of our attention for a few minutes on Sunday morning as part of a presentation to make us feel better, to help us feel closer to Him, or some other designed response, seems kind of odd, like we are putting God in a box to somehow serve us. That box is filled with emotionalism, intellectualism, or ritualism, and is all packaged in a convenient time frame. I wonder if God is not insulted by what we think is the ultimate way to pay tribute to him.

There is something more.

The Worship Principle

Worship has been associated with ancient rituals performed by ordained priests or ecstatic singing, praying, and utterances to be consumed by a congregation. In the minds of most people it is confined to a time (10:30AM) and a place (your local church). But what is it, really?

The word "worship" means to ascribe worth to an object. In the New Testament, the most frequently used word for worship is translated "worship" or "to bow down." Literally, it means, "to kiss toward." The idea is to show respect or reverence with the act of bowing. It is a visible act of love flowing from a heart of gratitude.

Another New Testament Greek word means to revere or adore. Yet another important word means service. It is the word from which the term liturgy is derived.

What can we learn from our brief look at these Greek words for worship? Worship is a two-sided coin. There is a spiritual/emotional aspect of awe and reverence to worship. But it also has a physical, action-oriented side.

Which one has received the majority of the attention for two thousand years? That's easy, the emotional, spiritual side. Not only that, but it has been relegated to a Sunday morning church service.

There are two very key passages that further explain worship.

A Samaritan woman that Jesus met at a community well was having a discussion with him about where was the best place to worship God, since the Samaritans and the Jews had different traditions. In John 4:24, Jesus indicated that true worship is in spirit and truth. The word for spirit literally means "wind." We use this word to describe tools that are powered by an air compressor as pneumatic. In this context, it may refer to the Holy Spirit or be a reference to our own spiritual nature. Most believe it is the latter.

So we worship God with our spiritual nature that he has given us (in spirit) and in accordance with the way things are (in truth).

There is a mystical side to worshipping God; after all He is spirit and we have a spiritual nature. This spiritual side is as valid as the truth/reality side of worship. It involves us ascribing worth to an infinite God, and sensing an affirmation that he is really there. It's hard to define or even describe, but it's real.

But we worship him in the context of everyday reality. We worship him the way he really is, rather than inventing a god of our making. We worship God in the real world, rather than in a fantasy world. We worship him in the context of our life, the way we really are, rather than pretending to be something we are not.

The next biblical text, Romans 12:1-2, answers the question, "What does God require of us?" It's a really good question, because throughout all of human history, people have been doing all manner of things in the name of God, including whipping themselves, offering animal, and even human sacrifices, depriving themselves, and even blowing themselves (and several "infidels") to smithereens, thinking this is want God wanted from them.

So, just what does he want?

Nothing. What could we possibly offer a God who loves us unconditionally and has redeemed us sacrificially? Over and over, Jesus makes the issue one of faith, simply believing him and believing he is who he said he was. Our relationship with God is not based on the barter system where we give him something in order to get something back in return. Every other religious system seems to be structured that way, but Christianity is different. God takes care of everything and leaves us dumbfounded. That very element, a thing called grace, has been a stumbling block to hordes of people throughout the centuries.

If we are in debt to God, or have to do something to garner his favor, the whole thing falls apart. God would not be omnipotent if we had to do something for him to accept us. He would not be unconditionally loving if we needed to do something in order for him to love us. He would not be the God of grace revealed in the Bible and in Jesus. He would be a god of our own making.

God has no requirements for forgiveness and acceptance other than belief; which means we give up on our attempts to try to get him to look favorably upon us. But there is a huge difference between a requirement and a response. Romans 12:1-2 reveals a response to God.

"And so, dear brothers and sisters, I plead with you to give your bodies to God because of all he has done for you. Let them be a living and holy sacrifice—the kind he will find acceptable. This is truly the way to worship him. " (Romans 12:1 NLT)

The very context in this passage is one of response, "....to give your bodies to God because of all he has done for you."

The response is physical and practical, because it involves our bodies. It is a living sacrifice, unlike the dead animal sacrifices of the Judaism of Jesus' day. So it is something we do with our life. It is holy, set apart to him. In other words, it is simply acting like Jesus who embodied God.

That is the response that God desires. It is acceptable. It is not a requirement. It a normal, reasonable response to what he has done for us.

Can you imagine a friend who says to you, "I will love you, if you …?" But what would be your response to a friend who loves you unconditionally, one who has seen you at your worst?

The word, "worship" in this passage is the one translated "service." So this kind of practical, living, physical service like that of Jesus is the very meaning of worship and it is a reasonable response to God's unconditional love.

Therefore helping out a neighbor in a jam is as holy as hymn singing, hand raising, praying, swaying, going to mass, or whatever. Probably, more so. It's God's way for us to "pay it forward," rather than keeping his good news to ourselves. And yes, it is real worship, as real as it gets.

While any way that we ascribe worth to God is worship, one of the purest ways is simply serving someone as Jesus would do.

Wide Open Worship

To review, there are two sides to worship; the mystical and spiritual side that stirs up feelings of awe and reverence, and the physical, action-oriented side that expresses your inner devotion through meaningful service. Worship is anchored in spirit and truth, but ultimately our worship is revealed in the way we live. That's what we learn from the Scriptures and it goes a long way beyond singing songs together once a week.

What triggers your desire to ascribe worth to God, to value God?

How about a walk around the lake in the peacefulness of nature, surrounded by the faint little sounds of insects, birds, and frogs? A hike through the woods, watching and listening to the critters stir ahead of you? A barefoot stroll in the surf of a vast sea with its magnificent waves, littered with shells that once housed all manner of small creatures? Maybe it is the multi-colored leaves, the clear blue skies, and crunching sounds underfoot on an October day. While you are out there, you may find yourself singing God's praise in your heart and maybe with your voice too.

Other people feel close to God while they ski down his slopes, surf his waves, climb his mountains, camp under his canopy, or fish his waters. The grandeur, diversity, and beauty of nature reveal the character of a God who is infinitely creative and has a love of beauty and fondness for variety. In the midst of your exhilaration, you might find yourself thanking God for the use of his playground.

God cares more about people that anything; that speaks of his patience. The shear diversity of humanity is pretty astounding. We come in all body types, speak an array of languages and dialects, have various skills, interests, and passions, and are so varied in our personality that no two people are alike.

I am amazed that God is interested in each one of us and has touched each life; all with different experiences, heartaches, and triumphs but with the same basic needs. We are each unique, yet similar.

Getting to know people is so fascinating. Sharing our heart with another person makes us feel connected and alive because our life only has meaning in the context of relationships and community. That makes me thankful that God created us for each other.

A visit to an art gallery, a concert, a well-crafted movie, a great story, all stir my soul on a deep level. Great art inspires me. Maybe this was someone's act of worship and now they have inspired me to pursue my personal act of worship through creating something. Indulge yourself in the arts and you will see God. The spark he put within you will be ignited. Don't worry if your creation is labeled "Christian" or not. The label isn't important to him.

We should become opportunistic worshippers, recognizing God wherever we find him. If we approach life like that, he will surprise us with a touch of the divine in weird and unlikely places.

I am a party worshipper. Yes, partying has been equated with binge drinking and irresponsible behavior, but that is a rip-off of a wonderful idea.

I would like to make partying a spiritual discipline, because it is absolutely healing for people to let their hair down, blow off some steam, enjoy great music, hang out with friends, and relax. Honestly, we need to party because Jesus is there at the party with us. He attended his share and I believe he had a good time. Relaxing and having fun together is healing. It reminds us of how God has created us for one another.

Music is an wonderful way to worship, but it doesn't have to be in a church service or Christian music to cause us to think about God, get lost in the moment, and be moved by its artistry.

Solitary reflection and prayer is a beautiful way that people have worshipped God down through the ages. I would highly recommend talking things over with God on a regular basis, purposefully examining our life, and remembering what he thinks about us. I need to do it on a regular basis just to keep the ship upright.

All of the ways to worship that I have mentioned are a means to get our batteries recharged and focus on God, but they don't require much of us. One aspect of worship sometimes requires a lot of us, but these opportunities deliver the best sense of touching the divine.

Just now, I am beginning to see that the various spiritual disciplines like Sabbath keeping, worship and service are not clearly delineated. They blur together. For instance, worship restores our soul and that makes it like keeping a Sabbath. But it also leads us to helping others and that makes it like service.

I am not even sure if these things should be called disciplines. Discipline is a good word in a way because it reminds us that doing these things make us better people. But it's a bad word in a way because it sounds like something we have to do, instead of a natural response to a loving God.

Back to worship. By most accounts, the very best sense of a divine connection comes from simply serving another person. It is a great feeling to help someone else, whether it is a homeless person who has nothing or a neighbor who just needs someone to talk to.

I plan on discussing this more later in the book, so I will just throw out the concept here. You don't need to save the world; instead just be free and willing to help your neighbor. Whatever type of service you choose to help your fellow man is great; however there is much to be said for just being available to family, friends, neighbors, and people who are normally in your world as opportunities spontaneously arise. Your world is probably composed of more people than you realize. If we are alert, we will see opportunities to serve people with whom we normally interact.

The key is to recognize the opportunity as a divine appointment and to be willing to be interrupted or to change your plans. These golden moments do not happen according to schedule and they can reveal themselves at inconvenient times. This kind of worship is messy because sometimes people try our patience and they don't usually get fixed just because we showed up.

This is worship...talking to a lonely acquaintance, shoveling snow for an elderly neighbor, watching a neighbor's house while he is away, being there for a family member when their world is shaken, reassuring an old friend who is struggling with haunting feelings of guilt, opening up your home to someone whose options have been exhausted, being an advocate for a person who can't do it themselves, and simply loving people unconditionally. The list is endless. Sometimes serving requires giving financial help and sometimes it is as small a thing as engaging in conversation.

Make no mistake, service equals worship. It ascribes worth to God when we are his Good News to other people, when we shine his light into the dark corners of life, bring a little hope, and show a little of his love.

three

An Ongoing Conversation

Prayer Performance Anxiety

Being a pastor can be a drag. There is this "man (or woman) of God" set of expectations that follows members of the clergy. Let me set the record straight; those in vocational Christian service, the ministry, clerics, whatever you want to call them, are as flawed as every other human being. Some of us, perhaps more than the average Joe.

A lot of pastors are co-dependent individuals who need to be needed by needy people. Some are adrenaline junkies who love being the go-to-guy. Some need to know they are loved and attempt to prove their worth by trying to fulfill the expectations of their congregants, and some are little tyrants. Many of them don't have anyone with whom they can be real. However, they all are frequently called on to pray as though it were a professional clerical function for which they have had some sort of special training enabling them to do it better than an untrained individual.

Pastors get called on to pray a lot. I never liked that any more than anyone else who gets called on to pray out loud. It's a huge responsibility to connect with the Almighty on behalf of several other people in a way that also connects with them. It's hard and takes some quick thinking or a slick (and often inauthentic) memorized prayer. Worse still, it seems to be an invitation to meet someone's expectations rather than simply and authentically communicating with God. It's like a celestial pop quiz. I often found myself unprepared, so I had to fake it.

Years ago, one really precious older church member, now deceased, recounted an account of my visit with his family member who was seriously ill in the hospital. He said that after I prayed with them (the family member and his loved ones who were there in the hospital room) there wasn't a dry eye. On the rare occasion of a respectable performance, or perhaps divine inspiration, my words apparently connected and touched the soul.

Prayer is commonly used as a way to help people feel better or to show them love. I suppose that's okay, but why not just say those things to them without the preface of, "Let's pray?" Maybe looking the person in the eye as we talk to God and them would be better.

I have even done prayer toasts at special family meals and it's kind of fun. If prayer is communication with God, then why are we so often focused on helping people feel better as we pray? Why do we say, "Let me pray with you," like we are about to cast some sort of magic spell?

Prayer for some people is going through a list of how you should pray. Each bead of the rosary reminds you of something, or an acronym such as ACTS (Adoration, Confession, Thanksgiving and, Supplication or asking on behalf of others) informs the movement of your prayers from topic to topic. I used that kind of format for a long time, but eventually I began wondering, "Why do I need a list of how to talk to someone who loves me unconditionally?"

Do you know what NPDA stands for? No Public Display of Affection. It's a way for fundamentalist Christians to try to keep their teenagers who are in love (or think they are) from constantly hanging all over each other in public. It helps the parents and the religious adults feel better. One can only imagine what's happening when the adults aren't around. Really, it is some sort of freakish, cult-like attempt to control normal behavior that forces adolescents into a duplicitous lifestyle, perhaps driving them in a direction their parents definitely would not approve.

But I digress.

When it comes to prayer, some Christians tend to have the opposite policy or PDA (Pubic Displays of Affection). The most common example I can think of is praying before meals in restaurants. All but the most seasoned of public pray-ers feel very awkward about this and it gets really weird when your server arrives in the middle of your prayer; which has happened to me countless times. But the custom is worn like a badge of piety by some believers. I just think it is awkward. Why not maintain an attitude of prayer, being grateful for your meal and your friend or whoever is joining you at the table. Like so many practices in the Christian faith, prayer is too intimate to be cheapened by some rote little display that we perform to get some sort of celestial badge of merit.

Public prayer is often used to sanctify events, like at dedications. I think it is often used in a perfunctory or manipulative way to gain respect from the local religious community.

If prayer really is conversation with God, then we don't need to choose our words carefully because he knows our heart and desires authenticity from us. We can say anything we want and sort through whatever is on our mind. But most prayer is not like that at all.

Some prayers are really sermons. You hear these at public events that involve politicians. Some people who have been called upon on these occasions have delivered some real doozies. Some are long lists of people with various physical ailments and it becomes a sort of PR thing, so you'd better not leave out anyone's name who is sick or on the prayer list. In some circles, prayers are unintelligible, supposedly spoken in a prayer language from the Holy Spirit. Some are full of the binding and loosing of the spirits, as though the person has mystical powers over the unseen realms.

Still, there is very little heart-to-heart talking with God.

For some people prayer is a magic pill, for some a ritual, for some a sermon. For some it's an excuse to revert to seventeenth century English, for some an opportunity to show off their eloquence or supposed spiritual powers, and for some it's a way to help people feel better. Are any of these real prayer, or are they an inauthentic prostitution of something highly personal, a meeting of the hearts of God and man?

The Prayer Principle

Virtually every religion practices prayer. Communicating with deity seems to be a nearly universal desire among humanity.

Prayer can be worship, confession, thanksgiving, or requests for ourselves, or others, or most anything one would want to say God.

Native Americans dance as a form of prayer. Hindus chant mantras. Jewish prayer may involve swaying back and forth. Muslims prostrate themselves on the floor or kneel. Quakers emphasize silent reflection.

There may be accompanying actions with prayer, such as anointing with oil, ringing a bell, lighting a candle, facing toward Mecca, making the sign of the cross, or fasting.

Payers are woven throughout the pages of the Bible. Abraham prayed for a son (Genesis 15:2). He also bargained with God to withhold his judgment on Sodom if he could find but a few righteous people who lived there (Genesis 18:23-24). Kings and generals prayed for victory in battle. The early Christian disciples prayed for boldness in the face of persecution (Acts 4:29-30). A thief on the cross next to Jesus prayed for mercy (Luke 23:42). David prayed a beautiful prayer of repentance (Psalm 51:10-13). Elijah prayed for both draught and rain, but not at the same time (James 5:17-18). Ezra confessed the sins of Israel (Ezra 9:6). Gideon prayed for a sign from God (Judges 6:36-38). Habakkuk prayed for justice (Habakkuk 1:2-4). Hannah also prayed for a son (I Samuel 1:11). Jabez prayed for prosperity (I Chronicles 4:10). A leper prayed for healing (Matthew 8:2). Moses prayed for water (Exodus 15:24). Paul prayed eloquently for the Ephesian Christians (Ephesians 3:14-21). He also prayed for deliverance form an undisclosed "thorn in the flesh" (2 Corinthians 12:7-10). Solomon prayed for wisdom (I Kings 3:6-9). A tax collector prayed for mercy (Luke 23: 39-43).

The Psalms contain as astounding breadth of prayers. You can find everything from requests to reign down judgment on enemies to lavish praise and desperate expressions of personal anguish. The Bible is full of examples of prayer, exhortations to pray, and assurances of God hearing our prayers.

Yet, prayer is a mystery. It seems like our prayers are only occasionally answered affirmatively. It leaves us scratching our heads in confusion, wondering if we prayed the right way, had enough faith, and asked for the right thing.

We pray for all manner of things from a good parking place to people being delivered from a fatal disease. Maybe we just don't understand God and the grand scheme of things, which gives him the latitude to answer our prayers yes, no, slow (not yet), and grow (there is a personal learning process involved). At least those are the list of options we have been able to come up with.

Actually, it seems strange that an omnipotent, omniscient, and omnipresent God would even want us to pray. Maybe he just likes hearing from us, or perhaps something else is in play.

There is so much that could be said or discussed regarding prayer, but I will focus on three important passages from the Bible.

The Lord's Prayer (Matthew 6:9-13 NLT) is perhaps the best-known passage on prayer. Rabbis had their own prayers that were embraced by their followers. This is Jesus'.

> Our Father in heaven,
> may your name be kept holy.
> May your Kingdom come soon.
> May your will be done on earth,
> as it is in heaven.
> Give us today the food we need,
> and forgive us our sins,
> as we have forgiven those who sin against us.
> And don't let us yield to temptation,
> but rescue us from the evil one.

This model prayer contains a reminder to regard God as holy or set apart from the world and the ordinary; that is worship. There is the pronounced longing for his rule and ways to prevail upon the earth; that is prophecy. Closely coupled with that is the expressed longing for his will to be done on earth; that is service, which places a responsibility upon the pray-er to do his part to make the world like it will be when ruled by Jesus.

There is a plea for sustenance and his provision of the necessities of life; that is dependence and a reminder that every good gift is from him. The plea for forgiveness is a recognition of our tendency to make decisions that dishonor him; that is confession. Interestingly, the plea for confession is tied to our forgiving people who have wronged us; that is forgiveness. The last plea of this prayer is to avoid the lure of temptation and the evil one; a plea for strength to avoid bad decisions and an admission of our weakness.

The overall mood of the prayer is one of dependence and humility as we ask God to help us keep our head and heart right.

There is a fascinating coupling of dependence and personal responsibility in the prayer, sometimes stated and sometimes implied.

He is holy. We should regard him as holy.

His kingdom is coming. We should be furthering his ways here and now.

We ask him to provide our basic needs. We have a responsibility to provide for our own physical needs (2 Thessalonians 3:10).

He forgives our sins. We forgive those who have sinned against us.

We ask him to protect us from temptation and the evil one. Implied elsewhere in scripture: We have personal responsibly to understand how temptation and the evil one work and to make responsible decisions (James 1:13-15).

I love the practicality of this prayer. It saves us from two extremes; acting like God doesn't exist and everything is totally up to us, or shirking our personal responsibility and essentially blaming God for what happens.

This is a beautiful prayer, repeated in many church services and that is fine. But it is a model for prayer. It is not a magical prayer. However, these are not the only words with which to pray and it must not become a mindless ritual. Other prayers in the Bible are very different from the Lord's Prayer. Remember, prayer is conversation with God. It would be more than a little odd if every time you talked to your husband or wife you followed a formula or said the exact same words.

The Lord's Prayer, which is really the disciples' prayer because it is for them (and us) giving us words to say when we don't know what to say; and they are beautiful words at that. It illustrates a balanced way to pray that can unite a group of people in prayer.

Moving from the beautiful to the confusing, we have to consider what Jesus said in Matthew 21:21-22 (NLT) because so many people get hung up on his words in this passage.

> Then Jesus told them, "I tell you the truth, if you have faith and don't doubt, you can do things like this and much more. You can even say to this mountain, 'May you be lifted up and thrown into the sea,' and it will happen. You can pray for anything, and if you have faith, you will receive it."

If we take these words at their surface meaning, we will simply believe you can pray for anything, and that if we have adequate faith, it will happen. If that doesn't sound quite right to you, it's because it isn't.

There are some problems with that interpretation.

It's hurtful. Imagine a mother praying for her sick child with all of her heart, but he dies anyway.

It doesn't align with what the rest of scripture teaches about prayer or real life situations in the Bible. For example, Paul prayed for deliverance from his "thorn in the flesh," but he was not healed.

As for moving mountains, I don't really think Jesus was encouraging us to try to alter topography. He was making a point by saying something ridiculous. His statement still has meaning, just not a superficial meaning.

He was saying you can pray about some really big things that seem impossible. They are not too big for God to deal with. It could be something like changing a mindset that someone has had all of their life or delivering you from an addiction that has a stranglehold on you. You know, big, impossible seeming stuff.

Then there is the faith thing. We need to believe he can do it. Usually, we are conflicted about this like the man who wanted Jesus to heal his son, who said, "I believe; help my unbelief." Sometimes we pray mostly believing that God can do something, but then we are surprised when he does. That's a normal human frailty.

The truth is that we can pray for something, have plenty of faith and it still not happen. That's because prayer is not about trying to twist God's arm. It's about us getting his perspective on things.

Honestly, this passage, like a lot of others, is difficult to understand.

The point is that prayer is not some sort of genie's lamp to rub and make a wish. It's something even better because we would make stupid wishes if the genie's lamp thing were true, since we don't see the whole picture. Instead, we can have honest and intimate conversation with our creator and redeemer, and gradually get our heart a little more aligned with his.

Chatting with God
It might go something like this.

> Well, good morning! I feel kind of scrambled today. My head is full of thoughts of things that need to be done and mental fragments that worry me. I wonder just where those dark thoughts come from and how I could possibly be so duplicitous. Thank you for that hint of

inspiration that makes me think you want me to be my truest, most honest and unique self. Anyway, with all of this going on in my head I need a major mental defrag and reboot.

As I look back over the last few days, it really hasn't been so bad. Some good things were accomplished and, though I slipped up here and there, I refuse to let those things define me. Help me to move on, knowing I am forgiven and could never have a relationship with you that was just based on my behavior anyway.

I definitely need your help with what I think the next few days hold.

Help me to get your perspective on those things that have troubled me lately. Help me to unconditionally love the people in my world, rather than try to change them. I hope each of them will catch a glimpse of how you love them and be inspired to love those around them in the same way.

Help me to keep pursuing my life's purpose, move toward excelling in loving people as they are, and remember to nurture my own soul.

For a long time, I used the A (adoration) C (confession) T (thanksgiving) S (supplication or asking on behalf of others) formula to guide my prayers. In the last few years, I have tried to stay away from formulas and opt for a more real expression of my thoughts, feelings, needs, and aspirations. I have come to believe that prayer is more for us than it is for you. While I think you must enjoy hearing from us, I realize you know our heart before we open our mouth or try to frame our thoughts with words.

So I worship you, not because you are a narcissistic deity, but because I am narcissistic person who needs a reminder that there is something, or rather someone, beyond me who is watching the store. That's both humbling and comforting.

I confess my sins to you, not as some sort of a magic formula to get you to forgive me for the stupid and hurtful things I have done, but rather to remind me of your forgiveness and who you are. I really ought to be giddy with grace, rather than plagued by guilt. You have given me the best motivation ever to avoid the stupid stuff, because you will keep on loving me the same no matter what. Help me to live out this truth in my life.

May I continue to pursue my truest core identity and purpose for being alive right here, right now. Help me to excel in loving people as they are and help to nurture my own soul with the enjoyment of all you have given me.

You can pray anywhere, about anything, at any time. It's a running conversation rather than a speech. It needs to be real and honest, balanced like the Lord's Prayer with dependence upon God and personal responsibility.

I start my day this way because I need to process all the scraps of thoughts floating around in my head. I need to be reminded of what God thinks about me. As the day goes on, often there is something that angers, frustrates, or confounds me. I am amazed at how quickly I slip into problem solving mode, or frustration, or anger. It is always better to stop and get God's take on things and maintain that balance of dependence and responsibility.

four

How Change Happens

You Need to Get Plugged-in

Confession: I am a dreamer, a planner, and an organizer. Some would add instigator and troublemaker to the list. Fifteen or so years ago, when our church was experiencing an amazing renewal after most of the old guard had bowed out, I was in a little zone that was a personal paradise. There was a fresh slate before me and I had some agreeable people to help me determine what the church was going to look like in the future.

We redesigned everything. It really needed it, but we went all the way back to a fresh slate. The building took on a new look. The ministry schedule and the very content of what we did was all new. We looked at basic purposes for the church and then "re-dreamed the dream" of what should and could be.

Nowhere was that more apparent than in the guiding documents of the church. We were radical, thoughtful, and ahead of our time in designing these. The Table of Contents of our Participating Members Manual was broken down into: Foundations, Statement of Beliefs, Membership, and Governance. The Foundations section breaks downs into: Mission, Values, Ministry, 10 Core Beliefs, 10 Core Virtues and 10 Core Practices. Here is a small sample. It seems too involved and contrived now, but we wanted to spell out exactly what we were trying to do.

Our Mission:
To help people reach their full potential in a relationship with God and each other

Our Values:
- Real. Accepting people as they are
- Relevant. Relating biblical teaching in a compelling manner.
- Relational. Encouraging relationships as the context for all we do.
- Rousing. Helping people awake to an intimate relationship with God.
- Reaching. Assisting people in moving toward their God-given potential
- (And, apparently, above all, being alliterative at all costs)

We even had a "six-step process that helps guide a person from being a pre-Christian to living a redeemed life of following Christ in responsibility and service."

All of that is an example of how today's church is infatuated with mission statements, defined processes, programs, classes, small groups, and services. It's hung up on the mechanics of discipleship. It's like a machine. You need to believe these things. You need to go to these classes. You need to serve in this way. The messages of the average church to a new person who happens to find their way to a service and break into the subculture of the church are something like this.

- We are so glad you are here. (We need a lot people to staff the church's programs and support it financially.)

- You need to get saved. (We won't really accept you until you declare your faith in Christ in a way that fits with our understanding and uses our terminology.)
- You need to get discipled. (We want to run you through a series of classes or groups that outline what we believe. When you sign off on all of that, we will accept you a little more completely.)
- You need to serve. (What we really mean is, support this church organization. We need a lot of volunteer staffers and money to keep this thing afloat.)

The modern church got stuck in a rut of presentations and programs. It is so stuck that when this methodology fails, they try to come up with better presentations (services) and programs (classes and small groups;) a strategy of relying on the same ideas, only trying harder.

I have four basic complaints about this approach.

- It treats people like cattle to be herded through a process with the other cows. That ignores one of the basic characteristics of God. He loves people, and people are all individuals. To treat everyone the same is stupid because they are at different places in their development and need different things to help them to continue to grow.
- It is knowledge-based, but gaining knowledge does not make us like Jesus. We might become better informed, but we may also become proud about the fact that we have the correct perspective on a doctrine while that of others is inferior. Scripture warns about knowledge leading to pride. It's a rampant problem throughout the church.
- It's the easy way out, avoiding the investment that goes into real spiritual formation. Sending someone to a

class is much easier than getting to know the person and sharing life with them.

- It ignores what God is doing. God is at work in everyone's life in a myriad of ways. It would be so much better to get to know a person, find out how God has been working in his life, and work together with him.

- It doesn't work. We have all kinds of resources available to us today, packaged programs, polished speakers, DVD's, downloadable sermons, podcasts, costly projection systems, and books upon books; but it doesn't seem to have really netted much improvement in the behavior of Christians.

One of the churches we attended after my pastoral years, had the 101, 201, 301, 401 class structure as their discipleship process. I had been a pastor for over two decades, but to be a member I had to attend their 101 class. I did. I hated it because I had taught those things for as long as some of the attendees had been alive. Before I attended 201, I was asked to teach 101. I declined.

This is not the way spiritual formation happens.

The Discipleship Principle

A disciple is a learner, follower, student, or apprentice. Jesus had seventy that he sent out on a mission trip in Luke 10 and, famously, there were twelve who were his closest associates who traveled with him for over three years. Peter, James, and John seemed have been part of his inner circle that was together with Jesus on numerous intimate occasions.

Jesus' registration process: "Come, follow me." His curriculum: life. His methodology: highly informal and interactive.

When Jesus was born, the people of Israel, especially those in the region of Galilee, were saturated with knowledge of the

Old Testament. They memorized large sections of scripture and debated its application.

The Mishnah is the book of rabbinic interpretations and oral traditions from 1BCE to 1CE. It helps us understand contemporary thought about spiritual formation during the time Jesus walked the earth. According to the Mishnah, at five, a Jewish boy was considered ready for the Scriptures, at ten, ready for the Mishnah, at thirteen, ready for fulfilling the commandments, at fifteen, ready for the Talmud (containing the opinions of the rabbis on thousands of subjects), at eighteen, the bridal chamber, at twenty, a vocation, and at thirty, authority or teaching.

Each community would hire a teacher (rabbi) who would teach the children the Torah (the foundational first five books of the Bible). It was like a religious elementary school. At some point, upon mastering the content, the children would stay home to help with the family business. Boys would learn the family trade, but the very brightest boys would continue their education with the rabbi. The most outstanding students would seek permission to study with a famous rabbi, usually leaving home and traveling with him. They were passionately devoted to their rabbi, noting everything he said and did.

Jesus was often called, "rabbi" because he fit the description of a first century rabbi, sought out by students, traveling from place to place, and dependent upon the hospitality of others. When the rabbi believed his disciples were prepared to be like him, he would commission them to become disciple makers themselves.

Sound familiar?

Jesus' way of spiritual formation took more than a few sterile class sessions using prepackaged materials. It took over three years, involved significant travel, teachings that seemed counter intuitive, misunderstanding, and difficult circumstances. It was not neat and tidy; it was life.

Jesus departed from the norm (as he did so often). Instead of having a band of the best and brightest as his disciples, he chose misfits, including a corrupt tax collector, a thieving anti-government terrorist, commercial fishermen with anger management issues, and a blowhard who was always saying the wrong thing. That's who he trained and to whom he handed over his mission. That's who paid dearly for their allegiance to him. That's who spread the revolution we call Christianity.

How can we summarize how Jesus developed disciples?

- He focused on small groups of people.
- He intentionally chose those people in whose lives he was going to make a major investment.
- He chose unlikely people, rather than individuals considered appropriate by society.
- He got burned. (Remember Judas.)
- They did life together.
- They experienced lighthearted moments together, as well as, times of intense stress.
- A lot of the time they misunderstood his teaching.
- They participated in the things he did.
- After an experience, he would ask them about it.
- Initially, they were very shaky, even though the mission depended upon them.

Helping People be Who They Are

Conventional church leadership wisdom says, "Build the church." That means to build the organization by increasing attendance, involvement, income, and influence. The discipleship process got morphed into teaching doctrines and trying to turn attendees into good church members, training newcomers to use their talents and gifts to sustain and expand the organization. That's church building, not spiritual formation.

It's selfish, but many well-meaning church leaders are innocently trying to build their church because they think that is the most important thing in the world. It's not; individuals are the most important thing in the world. People are the most important thing in the world, not organizations, not even the church.

We should change the question from, "How can we build the church?" to "How can we help a person reach their fullest potential?" That means we have to get to know them on a personal basis, rather than herd them through some program.

All of which puts us on a quest for something between a program-oriented approach that funnels everyone through the same classes, and just leaving them alone to figure it out on their own. Everybody needs some help and encouragement to be their own best selves. That takes us back to Jesus' method.

He did life with a small group of individuals. He spent extra time with just three people. That is how they learned, how they grew, how they found who they were. That is how they discovered their kingdom role.

How do we translate that to our culture? We are tied down with our tight schedules and are far less communal and more individualistic than the people in Jesus' culture.

Yet if people get together informally and spontaneously in small groups, the likelihood of real friendships and mentoring relationships developing is pretty good.

Churches could provide a great service if they trained and monitored mentors who would tag team with what God is already doing in a person's life, helping the individual take a step or two in fulfilling their potential. This would be a service the church could provide for those who want it. Maybe that is too programmed, but I think it would work if the mentors were carefully screened and trained, and facilitated and encouraged others instead of trying to direct their lives.

However, spiritual formation is not all relationally oriented. We are personally responsible for our own growth and nurture. I dealt with this to some degree when discussing how to have a Sabbath. There, I was talking about refreshment. Here, I am talking about spiritual formation. They are not as distinct as you may think.

We have to take care of ourselves, physically, mentally, emotionally and spiritually. Nobody else can or will do that for us, because it is our responsibility. If we don't do it, we will not be able to help other people or pursue our unique, personal contribution as we otherwise could.

Let's begin with what does not work well in the area of spiritual formation.

We cannot be taught into spiritual maturity. All of the classes and programs in the world will have limited, short-term results. They may inspire us. They may expose us to new information. We might add a new notebook to our bookshelf, full of new and exciting principles," but the affect of such things tend to be short-lived.

The nasty underbelly of gaining new knowledge about the Bible and the Christian life is that it tends to make us arrogant, so that we feel pretty special about having the knowledge and look down on others who do not.

Some segments of Christianity substitute knowledge for spiritual formation. Others confuse experience with true growth. On the Charismatic wing of the faith, people seek personal, supernatural manifestations from the Holy Spirit, such as speaking in tongues, being slain in the spirit, or some word of knowledge or wisdom. I understand these "manifestations" to be dubious, and possibly even dangerous. They can be misleading and lead to spiritual and emotional abuse. Just like the knowledge seekers, a person who has a special manifestation from God is something of a superstar. There are no superstars in Christ's kingdom, that's a human phenomenon.

How many times have you heard a program or retreat described as "life-changing?" People are so hungry and desperate, that "life-changing" sounds pretty good. Of course, the life change is short-lived and didn't really change your life. But some people are so desperate for something to fix their life or give them a deeper, more meaningful experience with God that they run to these things.

Spiritual formation is not knowledge and it is not power or experience. Spiritual formation is changing the way we think and the way we live our lives, and that is not easy. As a matter of fact, it's much easier to gain some new knowledge or to a have thrilling experience. However, those don't change our lives for the long term.

One more thing, the Christian life is not about self-reformation, though a lot of people think it is. So many Christians are trying to stop sinning, or at least sin less. They are struggling with something that repeatedly catches them in the same old trap. That's called addiction and it comes in more flavors than drugs, alcohol, and sex and it is universal in its appeal. There is something out there that entices each of us.

So that's their goal in life, to sin less, and it's an illusion. People who confuse being more like Jesus with sinning less are starting at the wrong place. They are trying to fix their life and the stuff they hate about themselves; but they can't.

It would be better if they started with Jesus and how he loves them even when they fail for the gazzilionth time. It would be better if they focused on how Jesus loved misfits. Then we could learn how to love other misfits and people with "issues."

Over time, desires will slowly change. We learn a little more about how to love others and ourself. We don't go nuts when we fail; we confess it and stay the course. Our desire for the prostitution of God's good gifts diminishes, because we are focused on something so much better.

What does this life change look like? It looks like love, grasping how God loves me, loving him back, and loving the people I encounter in my life in tangible, meaningful ways.

To the best of my knowledge, there is no definitive answer to the question, "What changes our life for the better?" But here is what I do know.

People inspire people. Programs seldom do. I remember teachers who were passionate about their subject and caring toward me more than I remember the subject matter they taught. Helping people reach their potential is a highly interactive pursuit. It requires people to trust each other and be transparent with one another. It means being around as things come up in life. It is very messy and, at times, totally frustrating.

Stories touch hearts and minds. Information seldom does. Stories make us human. They help us understand how ideas and opinions developed. They give us something we can relate to and they hold our attention. Reframing facts into stories is just good teaching methodology.

Change happens because we decide to change, not because someone or something outside of us tries to change us. People don't change because of a class or retreat, not for the long term. Each person determines his own mindset. Granted, life circumstances can force our hand and cause us to feel we must change or to believe we can change, but it is all deeply personal. Nobody can possibly do this for us.

Change is gradual, rather than dramatic. All of those testimonies of God miraculously, instantaneously delivering people really mess with our minds and cause us to think something is wrong with us. However, those cases of instantaneous change are the very rare exception. They are usually told right after the big change, before the person has had much of an opportunity to stumble again. Here's reality. Life is composed of forward steps, backward steps, and just staying the course.

It's always great when the general course of your life is positive, but that's not always the case. You will go off course, fall off the wagon, stumble, whatever you want to call it. One of the real signs of maturity is not sulking and staying there.

Maybe I am focusing on the wrong thing. Why worry about change? Why not just learn to love Jesus and understand how he loves us? Why not just focus on the relationship, on falling in love, rather than a list of things that are supposed to make the relationship better? Perhaps that is a more pure and succinct way of describing how spiritual formation happens.

five

People Who Need People

Forced Together

Perhaps the best (and worst) thing about being a pastor is the people. Maybe everyone could say the same thing, not just pastors and church-going folks. But pastoring a small church is relationally intensive. I love so many of the friends I made in those years as a pastor, but a small church is a family and all families have a weird uncle.

Churches attract weird people, and some relatively normal ones too. However, some people go to church with unrealistic expectations of having their needs met, or with the unexpressed desire for some well-intentioned people to enable their unhealthy behavior.

I have had people in my house after midnight, people consuming hours on the phone, and people lined up at my office door late at night, all telling me about their problems. Some people were stuck trying to figure out their marriage. Some were looking for someone to take their side in a relational dispute. Some were experiencing chronic emotional issues, but didn't want to do what they needed to do to get better. Some just wanted to complain about something. Some were mentally ill. Some were just going through a rough patch and needed a sounding board. I could tell you some stories about people that would make you laugh and cry, and surprise and shock you, but I don't want to get sued, so we will move along.

I am just going to blurt this out: some people are a lot harder to like than others. Some folks are generally delightful. There are a few people you can really identify with and you just click; others get on your nerves. There are those people whose self-consumed personalities simply suck the oxygen right out of the air and you know it will always be a one-sided relationship. They're takers.

Unfortunately, a lot of pastors and church people feel they have to not only love, but also like everyone. That's a big mistake because some people are asses. Sometimes, I'm an ass!

It would be ultimately disrespectful to ourselves, others, and God himself to like everyone, but we tend to feel guilty when we can't pull off this "sweet Christian that just loves (and likes) everyone" act. Don't.

In recent years, I have given myself freedom to not like everyone, not trust everyone, and not want to be marooned on a deserted island with just anyone. It's okay.

Another crazy idea that church people have is to try to mix people up so they can get to know one another. Churches do this by assigning people to small groups. While there is some benefit to getting to know a diverse group of people, relationships can't be forced.

One church I was a part of in my post-pastoring years, had us running across the county to meet with people who lived in other communities. We had little in common and it became stressful to go.

You can introduce people to each other, but you can't engineer relationships.

More than any other factor, relationships are why people stay in or leave a church. No matter how good church services and programs are, without relationships it becomes perfunctory.

It funny how we just click with some people, enjoy their company and honestly help each other. It's also mysterious. I think the Holy Spirit is involved in that.

The Community Principle

The Christian community, whether a specific local church or the church at large in the world, is understood to be "the church." It's confusing because people speak of their church, the specific one they attend. They speak of the church in their city with all of its manifestations and they speak of The Church or all Christians around the world. Often people refer to the building where the programs of the church take place, or even their denomination, all with the same term "church."

The English term, "church" comes from a Greek work used only twice in the New Testament. It means "belonging to the Lord." So, all of the people who "belong to the Lord," are the church.

The more common Greek word used in the New Testament is *ekklesia*. It is a compound word meaning, "out" and "to call or summon." Hence, the idea of an assembly called out for specifically Christian purposes.

There are three ways this word is used in the New Testament. It can refer to any assembly, gathered for any purpose. Or it can refer to a particular local church or have the more universal meaning of the church around the world.

There are also metaphors in the New Testament used to describe the church, like, the body of Christ, the bride of Christ, the temple of God, the building of God and the flock of God. All have the idea of a community of people belonging to God and representing him on earth.

The church was a new thing, marking a huge transition from the way we see God at work in the Old Testament. There, he had a representative people, an ethnic group, the Jewish people. In the New Testament, He also has a representative people, but not an ethnic group. Instead, the church was intentionally composed of people from all ethnicities right from the start.

Most biblical scholars understand the church as first coming about after the ministry, death, and resurrection of Christ, because those events are foundational for the church. Christ opened the door to a connection with God that was more obviously egalitarian than the way his chosen people of the Old Testament represented Him.

Scholars understand the birthday of the church to be the Day of Pentecost, as described in Acts 2. It was one of the Jewish feasts celebrating the harvest, so Jewish people from all over the known world would have been in Jerusalem. The Apostle Peter began to preach to the crowd about Jesus and how prophecy was being fulfilled. As he preached, everybody miraculously heard him in their native tongue. The Holy Spirit then came in a new, more sustained, and intimate way to live within believers. That's the church's birthday.

Immediately after this account in Acts 2, is a beautiful description of a community coming together to worship God and share their possessions and life itself with one another. Some people believe this passage to be the purest description of what the church should be like.

Persecution of Christians began almost immediately by the Jewish authorities and then the Romans, so Christians had to band together for their own safety. They also needed to share their resources.

The church that had begun as an underground movement, rapidly spread throughout the world and suffered a long period of persecution and internal debate until Constantine created the Holy Roman Empire in the fourth century. That ushered in about six centuries of Christendom.

The church and government became entangled and a huge source of power in the world. The eastern and the western church split in 1054. Protestantism began in 1517, with a call back to the basics of the gospel and scripture. Then various Christian sects seeking more freedom from state churches and oppressive governments helped to found America.

Along the way, institutions developed, hierarchies were formed, more and more divisions happened in the name of righteousness, and the church developed some serious baggage. Today there are power struggles, Christian celebrities, jobs and doctrinal positions to protect, subcultures within subcultures, Christian branding for books, music and other products, and, most dangerously, there is pride that comes from each group believing they are right.

That's the church. It's messy.

Let's try to get back to the core of it all. The church is a community of people representing God and the good news about Jesus to the world.

There are two pieces to this definition. One is mission oriented, representing God to world. Most Christians would understand that to be a combination of the Great Commission (making disciples of all people or ethnicities,) and the Great Commandment (loving God and our neighbor).

The other part of the definition is about community and relationships.

Normalizing Community

My basic sticking point with the institutional church is that it doesn't seem real! It's separated from regular life! It's internally focused upon growing the organization or, at least, trying to sustain it, rather than being focused on its mission. That mission is largely external and carried out in the context of relationships. This is where the church comes up short precisely because there is so much emphasis on maintaining the organization.

When something becomes an institution you have to continue to feed it. In the church's case, it takes people and money to keep things going. Institutions are like that. They begin with a specific function to somehow serve people, but as time goes on, they become more powerful. As they grow, they create an infrastructure that has to be maintained, so that eventually the institution moves from serving the people to the people serving it. It's gradual, it's subtle, but it's not hard to find examples. The church is one of them, and it has some serious baggage acquired over two millennia.

As I wrote earlier, the reason most people stay a long time at a church or leave it is relationships. At least some church leaders try to foster relationships, because they understand this truth. Yet it seems that things inevitably revolve around the needs and programs of the church. In fact, sometimes, good relationships do develop in that context. If you do anything together with other people, relationships will develop. But it seems like the tail is wagging the dog.

Relationships may happen in the context of church programs, instead of relationships being the context for everything, but the church uses people for its organizational purposes rather than helping them reach their potential.

If you have allegiance to a church organization, you have special church activities and church friends, and then you have the real world stuff. The whole movement that I support calls for normalizing the faith and the church, setting faith right in the middle of regular life, mixing up life and faith so they are a blend, rather than keeping them as separate elements.

The defenders of the institution have an arsenal of objections to this kind of faith expression.

"You can't be a lone ranger Christian. You have to have community with other believers. I agree, but I define community differently than they do. They think of community as gathering a large group of people together, looking at the back of each other's heads, singing songs and hearing sermons. I define it as sharing a slice of life with another person. One happens at ten am on Sundays in a special building; the other can happen anywhere and at any time. One requires an organization; the other simply requires an awareness of the people around you.

"You need some accountability." Usually, the church is not very good at providing accountability, because they don't know people well enough to even know what goes on in their lives. A few cultish churches carry it too far and try to control people's lives in a judgmental, graceless sort of way.

Accountability needs relationships. I have accountability because I have a wife, I have children, I have neighbors and I have associates. It is those relationships that keep me from taking a jump off the high dive of life into the deep end of irresponsible behavior.

"You need the teaching, strength, and support of a group of believers." I need to learn how to live so much more that I need some sterile class or sermonic exhortation. Following Christ is something that happens in life, not notebooks. I only wish that the church did a decent job of providing support. Occasionally, it does, but usually it does not. You don't generally get much personal support from an organization.

But what does this "free range faith" this "being the church, rather than going to church" look like? How can it have a relational aspect?

First, there is a responsibility aspect to it. Once, you decide to no longer outsource your faith expression to an organization of a professional; it becomes a personal choice.

Second, there is a relational aspect. You assume a new responsibility to focus on the people in your world by taking time to notice them, engaging with them whenever you can, loving them unconditionally and being there for them when they have a need. (I know, it's easier said than done.)

Your church just became all of the people in your world. You get to show them a little bit of Jesus, but you also get to be yourself. We don't need any more phonies pretending to be spiritual giants, because there are no spiritual giants. There are only people who love and want to live life in the way of Jesus, who once in a while happen to get it right.

You are not trying to get anyone to go to church or join a group. You are just trying to love them. The way you do that is wide open.

Think about the people in your life that you want to love and influence. That list would likely include your family, friends, neighbors, and associates. Then think about how to love them. It will be different for each person, but unconditional love is the core.

Pay attention to every person you encounter in the course of a day. Give each one your undivided attention. Give them a little love. At least, that's what I try to remind myself to do.

This way of being the church is so normal. It's part of life. Relax. Just love people.

It can get messy, because people are messy. It won't follow much of a schedule. Loving people like this is a mindset, not a program.

But it's fun. You get to know a lot of different kinds of people, and see the various ways God is at work in their lives.

Besides, we are made for relationships. We are made to love and it's very rewarding.

I almost got away with it, but I can't do it in good conscience. I almost left out the biggest thing that keeps us from having more meaningful relationships. There are some people we really don't want anything to do with, not because of their weird personality, but because of something within us that causes us to avoid large groups of people due to no fault of their own.

There is an innate tendency for human beings to label other human beings. Here I will use religious labels, but they could also be ethnic or socio-economic labels.

Labels are good on cans, but bad when applied to people. Canned goods are simpler and purer than people, tomatoes means tomatoes and beans means beans. You are able to determine what is in the can by its label. When you get home from the grocery store, you can put all of the beans together on one shelf in your pantry and all the diced tomatoes on another.

When we apply labels to people, the same thing happens. We put all the Christians together on one shelf in our mind. Then whatever our impressions are of Christians gets applied to everyone we slapped that label on. Our mental pantry of religiously labeled people might look something like this.

- Christians: arrogant, conservative in their politics, family people (not gay, not single), middle class, white, bigots
- Muslims: terrorists (or strangely silent on the matter), gas station/convenience store owners and managers, not the cleanest
- Buddhists: bizarre beliefs about reincarnation and karma, weird, lazy, fair game for jokes
- Atheists: heathen, cold, belligerent, destroying our nation's Christian foundation

Once the label is applied, a person is put in their appropriate place in our mental pantry. Then we apply all of the adjectives (usually negative, always sterotypes) that go along with that group to that person. Now we no longer need to think of the person as an individual, but we simply identify them as Muslim, Christian, or whatever. It's stereotyping or religious profiling.

While labeling makes our lives simpler, it shrivels our minds and hearts, causing us to deprive ourselves of getting to know people on an individual level.

Labeling also keeps us from finding truth and beauty in people and places that seem unlikely to us to possess any truth or beauty. But truth and beauty are all over the place, especially in unlikely people and places. So even very flawed religions (and they all are) can give something to the world. Buddhism has a reverence for life and central value of doing no harm. Islam is a religion that places high value on living out its beliefs through obedience. Even atheism brings a perspective of careful analysis and personal responsibility for one's beliefs and values.

Erin, a long distance, Internet friend and the editor of my book, *An Irreligious Faith,* claims to be an atheist. She has returned to college to earn a social work degree and fulfill a passionate desire to do what she can to help disadvantaged people. Erin is kind, encouraging and a good writer and thinker. She is not militant about her atheism and I am not militant about my beliefs.

The labeling thing is personal with me. Politically, I lean liberal on some things, and conservative on others, but mostly I think our political system is terribly broken. I despise listening to people who only repeat political party talking points from either side. It irritates me when people spout off with a knee jerk reaction on an important issue without giving it careful consideration or listening to someone who has a different perspective.

I am a person of faith who pretty much hates religion, so I'm hard to label, yet I get labeled all the time. I don't like it, because it's not fair to me. Labeling is not fair to anyone.

Our task is to love people, not to categorize or judge them.

six

Do You Have a Moment?

Excelling at Enabling

We meant well. We were a young upstart church, determined to do things differently. If a person came into the church with a physical need, we wanted to help out.

Before I go on, I need to explain a few things. Churches are targets for those who choose to live from hand-out to hand-out. There are people who are experts at working the system, manipulating people, and preying upon the good-heartedness of Christian people. They would come to our church door all the time.

The plea would be, "I just need some money for...." (fill in the blank.) They would throw in a few Christian catch phrases, and try to act humble. Usually, when they found out we only made out checks to specific creditors, the person would get up and leave, often saying bad things about our Christian faith on the way out as one last ploy to prey upon our guilt.

We were not staffed to either investigate or respond to such needs. Most churches are not. We did, however, support a local organization formed for this very purpose. They would investigate the need to see if it was legitimate. If it was, they would network with churches to meet it.

In our naïve ambition we decided to things differently. We had a volunteer who was responsible to investigate and respond to people who presented with physical (usually financial) needs.

Our church attracted down-and-out kind of people. I was really proud about it; because that's the way I believe the church should be. After a while, we already had so many needy people among us that we had our hands full and our budget maxed out.

There was a very cool element to our church in that era. If someone had a need, and someone else or a group of people could meet it, it was taken care of spontaneously and without fanfare.

The downside was that the people we were helping were repeat customers. They didn't do the things they needed to do to get to a better place. We worked with them to help them develop their own plan to improve their situation, but they usually did not follow through, even though we provided every kind of support possible. We became great enablers, inadvertently supporting people's irresponsible behavior.

Another thing we did was called random acts of kindness. A good friend of mine coordinated this ministry. We gave out bottles of water at baseball games, paid people's tolls on the tollway, had a free carwash, and hosted a dinner for neighborhood businesses.

This stuff is fun because it surprises people and makes them curious.

This type of service represents a marked change in the way Christians reach out to the community. It was a switch from the "come and hear" approach that Christians use to try to get people to come to their services and hear their pastor preach. On the other hand, it represents an honorable tradition of Christians historically being at the forefront of meeting human need on a global scale.

A huge portion of the hospitals, orphanages, and charitable organizations around the world had their origins in an expression of faith to care for the "least of these." If not for these Christian organizations, even more vulnerable people would have been totally disregarded by society.

Unfortunately, many Evangelical Christians became totally concerned with the "spiritual status" of a person, while ignoring their physical needs. Their concern was with telling them the Gospel about how Jesus died for their sins, and the need to get saved. Then the person needed to acknowledge that fact in prayer, go through the rite of baptism, and continue to grow as a Christian through Bible study. We called it evangelizing; a word that refers to a good message or good news.

But our little church decided, as have a fair portion of evangelicals, to be good news, rather than just verbalize it. The idea of preaching at people is rather distasteful to most everyone. Christians' credibility is so awful; we must live out our faith, rather than just try to verbally force it on people. I think that was the way it was always meant to be.

Therefore, there is no real line between evangelism and service. It's a matter of representing God to others, especially to those who think he has forgotten about them.

The Service Principle

The idea of focusing on others and their needs is probably as old as humanity. For Christians, the principle is most succinctly stated in The Great Commandment, loving our neighbor as ourselves (Matthew 22: 36-40). Jesus boiled the whole faith down to loving God and loving people and, specifically, loving our neighbor as ourselves.

Strange how the very core of what it means to live in the ways of Jesus as a child of God could be so often overlooked, while Christians focus on the minutiae of doctrinal detail. Really, how ironic is that?

Even in the Old Testament there were provisions made for the poor, including the practices of gleaning (leaving portions of the fields unharvested so the poor could have some grain for their survival) and almsgiving (giving to those who had no option other than to beg for the necessities of life).

Yet one of the most inspiring motivations for compassionate service is the very life of Jesus. He seemed to love hanging out with the outcasts of his day. You could make a long list; a Samaritan woman, an adulteress, a cheat of a tax collector, a terrorist supporter, a prostitute, lepers, the disabled, a Roman soldier, beggars. These were people who were either completely disregarded or fervently hated.

In Matthew 25:35-40 he connects our treatment of the needy, the hungry, the stranger, the destitute, and the imprisoned to how he will judge us.

In the story of the Good Samaritan (Luke 10:30-37) he masterfully reveals how someone who really loves will extend a helping hand to hated outcasts and enemies. But he also exposes the tendency of the religious to be so preoccupied with their responsibilities that they literally pass by an injured man in need of medical care.

In James 1:27; 2:15-16 we find that genuine faith will result in caring for those who have no one else, like widows and orphans. Real faith will result in real action for those who have real physical needs.

Even today, hundreds of charities founded as Christian organizations distribute billions of dollars worth of goods and services to those who most need them all over the world.

The very core of the faith is altruistic, serving people with no thought of reward.

The unique thing about Christian service is its scope. There are many organizations and religions that have some sort of charitable response for its adherents in place. The Christian tradition reaches out to believer and non-believer, people of other cultures, and those marginalized by society.

Service flows from love, and love is a tricky thing. At times it seems like an emotion, and other times, a hard choice or a sacred commitment. It grows through time as we experience someone loving us no matter what and we begin to love others in the same way.

In the summer, my wife sells her handcrafted jewelry at a large farmers' market on the Lake Michigan waterfront.

One Saturday last summer, a neighboring vendor asked if I could come help an elderly gentleman who had fallen. Probably his walker had a wheel go off the sidewalk and that caused him to take a tumble. As I approached him, he lay on the ground with his walker underneath his legs. He was probably 85 – 90 years old, out on a beautiful day to take in the market with his wife who had driven them there. They were extremely gracious Italian Americans who spoke broken English.

Even though I had just met them, I really liked them.

We helped the gentleman up so he could sit on the seat of his walker and I got a chair for his wife who was the more shaken of the two. Wonderful people gathered around to help. The paramedics were called, as was their son. The elderly man was checked out and deemed to be okay. The delightful couple was driven home by their son.

It did my heart so much good to help someone in need, but I was fighting back the tears the whole time (as I am now) for two reasons.

Their age and condition so parallels that of my parents and that really got to me emotionally.

Also, that very day was our fortieth anniversary. Patty and I were so young when we got married that we grew up together, and now, we are growing old together.

I was thinking that in 20-30 years we will be in a similar condition as this frail, yet loving, elderly couple.

I have personal experience with the helpless feeling of watching Patty fall and not be able to get to her in time. I watched her struggle with intense pain until she had her knee replaced and then witnessed her long recovery process.

As I tried to help the gentleman and his wife, I was thinking about an elderly version of Patty and me; then tears really welled up in my eyes.

The old man trying to reassure his wife and everyone else that he's okay, the old woman whose heart is broken by her husband's fall; that is what love is like.

Just Help People

Sometimes we all get lost in our own little fantasies. A lot of them can be prefaced with "I should have said" or "Here's what I would really like to tell them." I had a writing assignment for a magazine based on just that type of fantasy.

Before you read it, I should probably say that we really shouldn't do this kind of thing because people can't take the truth and we shouldn't try to force it on them, especially in large doses. Love's more effective.

And now I feel like I've issued enough disclaimers to let you read this imaginary last sermon.

(Sigh) I'll just get right to it!

Today I am tendering my resignation as your pastor.

This will be my last month with the church as I help the

board through the transition process, assuming they still want me to stick around after I finish this sermon.

I realize this news may be a shock to many of you, though perhaps some of you will be relieved that I am stepping down. I have no axe to grind with any particular individual, but I can no longer support a broken institution.

The church's focus has shifted from following Jesus to supporting an organization. When leading an organization, you have to feed it with increased attendance, finances, and volunteer staffing.

Some of you are diehard supporters of this church and have held sway over it with little regard for those who are uninitiated to its ways. Yet those are the very people we should be blessing. So, I am casting my lot with them.

As Christians we should be known by our love, not our hate, so I am trying to love those who have been rejected by the church. Admittedly, I have some catching up to do.

Instead of serving you and providing all kinds of ministries for you, I should have been equipping you to live in the real world where you could actively love people like Jesus did. So I am turning away from pandering to those who should know better, to simply loving those around me.

In our attempts to be relevant and cool, we have spent thousands of dollars to attract people to this building. We should be going and showing, instead of asking people to come and hear. Our "coolness factor" is nothing compared to honesty, acceptance, and love.

The church needs to become the center of the community and actively display Christ's love through activities that bless the people of the community. It should be the busiest building in town.

When you say, "Just preach the word, brother!" I fear you mean, "Repeat my theology back to me in an intellectual, but understandable manner so I will feel satisfied that I have it right. Then I can look down on the heretics."

I will not do that anymore. I believe in a God who is mysterious and I believe that people should have the freedom to ask questions and express doubts.

Instead of trying to make our congregants happy by serving up a smorgasbord of programs, we should be trying to figure out how to love the people in our community.

You have expectations of my wife that are far and above that of other members. You tell me when my kids are expressing themselves in normal adolescent ways, as though they should be above that. You even want us to dress a certain way. I am done playing that game.

I realize my lack of inhibition this morning has likely caused those of you who don't like me to change your feelings to something more extreme. That's up to you. What's up to me is to not harbor bitterness and to be true to my heart. I am working on both points.

Whatever you think of me, I hope that you love the church and the one who heads it enough to consider what I have said today.

While this imaginary sermon is pretty all-inclusive and bit brutal, it does illustrate the tendency for the church to become internally focused while people all around us need to see our faith in action.

Living out your faith is not rocket science. You don't need somebody to tell you how to do it. You certainly don't need an organization or a program in order to be loving and caring toward people. You simply need to realize it's up to you and then live your life with your eyes open, noticing the people and opportunities all around you. Oh yeah, you need to be willing to be interrupted and you need to really love people so that you don't think of them as projects.

You will need to say goodbye to your comfort zone. Serving, loving, and relating to people like Jesus did will take you places you have never been. That's because with Jesus there are no untouchables, no outcasts, no fringe, no minorities, no ethnicities, no unacceptable people. Actually, he sought them out; or they sought him. These folks need to see a little of Jesus' love and we can be the ones who have that honor.

You might need to reach out to someone you don't like or someone you would not normally associate with. You might find yourself called on to enter a whole new arena when you begin to help a person.

You will need to get some "new glasses" so you can begin to see people that you never noticed before. That's what is so impressive about Jesus; he noticed people who were invisible, when everyone ignored them (or hated them); people like a blind beggar, a leper, or a Samaritan woman.

We encounter a lot of people in our regular life. Most of them we don't think about; they are just there. They perform a service and then we go on. We need to start thinking about them and engage them as the opportunity presents itself.

We need to expect to be interrupted. Opportunities, needs, and crises never happen at a convenient time. There is a time to forget about our priorities and just be available to help someone. This is a hard lesson for me.

It's not love until we get moving. Warm feelings and well wishes fall short. Love requires things of us.

A lot of people find meaning in participating in organized efforts that help people, like a food kitchen, homeless shelter, or some other endeavor. That's great, because then you have the opportunity to experience community with the other people involved in serving. But you don't need an organization to care about people; you just need to be aware of the opportunities around you.

seven

Let It Go

We Will Now Receive an Offering

When I was a pastor, occasionally someone would wisecrack, "Do something religious. Take an offering."

Supporting the local church and other ministries with your time, talent, and treasure has always been a part of church tradition. These things take money, lots of money. There are mortgages to pay for the buildings, utilities and maintenance for upkeep, salaries and benefits for the staff, supplies for the programs, and a share for the denomination and other ministries. That's a lot of money.

That's just the average local church. How many churches are there in your city? There are also large ministries, many of them charitable, that take in huge sums. Of course, there are also a few charlatans living large off of the donations of their followers, but most churches and ministries are just trying to keep the bills paid.

Church leaders understand the church to be the means through which God works today and they believe their church is part of that. Doing church in the modern age takes money or so the reasoning goes. Therefore, they can in good conscience ask the flock to fund their needs. Most churches and Christian organizations manage their finances carefully and responsibly.

The most faithful of church members regularly give a predetermined percentage of their income. The term "tithe," means one tenth and is held up as the model for giving. (More about that later.) Church leaders dream of what they could do if everyone in the church tithed.

Like a lot of churches, we downplayed the offering by prefacing it with, "The offering is for our regular members who call this church home. If you are a guest today, please don't feel obligated to give. We want this service to be our gift to you."

I liked that because it surprised people and destroyed the stereotype that the church is after your money. But make no mistake, churches live or die (literally) by the offering.

The Giving Principle

Churches didn't just come up with the offering idea as a way to keep things going. The idea of religious donations has a long history.

Tithing, or giving one tenth of your income, is a very ancient practice, even predating the Mosaic Law. Abraham tithed to the mysterious King Melchizedek and Jacob promised to give God a tenth of everything when he had a vision at Bethel. In the Pentateuch the tithe is presented as a way of supporting the Levites and priests, who were unable to provide for themselves because of their religious duties.

There were also other tithes and offerings prescribed, so that ancient Israelites were probably giving more like twenty-five percent of their income for religious purposes. It would be given in the form of grain, animals, and produce.

An important thing to remember is that ancient Israel was a theocracy, a rule by God, as it were. So supporting their religion and its "clergy" was also supporting the government. It was like paying your taxes, and just like paying our taxes, it wasn't optional.

Through the ages, governments have found ways to demand a tithe from its citizens, and some governments still collect a church tax to support government-approved churches, usually around 1-2% of income.

Unfortunately hordes of pastors through the ages have equated their local church with the ancient Jewish Temple to try to keep the concept of tithing alive. That is a gross, but common, abuse of the text.

Malachi 3:8-12 (NLT) is a popular go-to text to support tithing.

"Should people cheat God? Yet you have cheated me! But you ask, 'What do you mean? When did we ever cheat you?' You have cheated me of the tithes and offerings due to me. You are under a curse, for your whole nation has been cheating me. Bring all the tithes into the storehouse so there will be enough food in my Temple. If you do', says the LORD of Heaven's Armies, 'I will open the windows of heaven for you. I will pour out a blessing so great you won't have enough room to take it in! Try it! Put me to the test! Your crops will be abundant, for I will guard them from insects and disease. Your grapes will not fall from the vine before they are ripe,' says the LORD of Heaven's Armies. 'Then all nations will call you blessed, for your land will be such a delight,' says the LORD of Heaven's Armies."

Preachers love to equate not tithing with cheating God, while promising blessings to the tithers.

Jesus had a different take in Matthew 23:23-24.

"What sorrow awaits you teachers of religious law and you Pharisees. Hypocrites! For you are careful to tithe even the tiniest income from your herb gardens, but you ignore the more important aspects of the law—justice, mercy, and faith.

You should tithe, yes, but do not neglect the more important things. Blind guides! You strain your water so you won't accidentally swallow a gnat, but you swallow a camel!"

He condemns the meticulous and legalistic mindset of the Pharisees who were great at tithing, but lousy at practicing justice, mercy, and faith, which are of considerable greater importance.

When you get into the New Testament letters, most of which were sent to churches in various locations in the Roman Empire, there is a marked absence of exhortations to tithe. But there are instructions about giving.

The most complete of those New Testament instructions lies in 2 Corinthians 8-9. Paul is encouraging the church in Corinth to give to support the persecuted and struggling Christians in Jerusalem. He refers to the church at Macedonia as an example in the way they supported them.

The Macedonians were actually poor themselves, yet they gave willingly and generously above what they could afford. He said they gave out of love, exceeding all expectations. They truly were cheerful givers. They considered helping these needy people a privilege. As a result of their generosity, he writes, many people will thank God. He mentions how this kind of generous outpouring has its origins in the grace of Jesus, who gave up so much for us so we could experience his riches. The Apostle Paul never gets heavy handed with the Corinthians or tries to pressure them. He simply cites the beauty of how the Macedonians gave.

From a practical perspective, he encouraged people to give based on what they have. The amount is not a one size fits all kind of thing. It's individually and privately determined, proportionate to one's personal financial situation.

The Apostle John makes the connection between love and charitable action. In 1 John 3: 17-18 (NLT).

"If someone has enough money to live well and sees a brother or sister in need but shows no compassion—how can God's love be in that person?

Dear children, let's not merely say that we love each other; let us show the truth by our actions."

Expressing our faith through giving is a personal thing, determined by the need, and our own ability. Yet a selfless, generous gift, given cheerfully out of a loving heart, is a beautiful thing that honors God and encourages others.

Fun with Money (and Stuff)

Giving money and possessions to others is a sign that our heart is in the right place.

Paying our bills is good too and an important responsibility. When we are trying to sort out our finances, that's the obvious place to start. Maybe we can lower our bills. Also good.

I was never very good at long-term financial goals, but paying for your kids' education or funding your retirement requires a very long-term approach. The earlier you start, the better. These days, I believe one of the best things Patty and I can do is to build up that neglected retirement fund, so we won't have to be dependent on the government or our children to provide for us in our golden years.

Then we get to a whole discretionary area; what to do with what's left over. Paying ahead on a bill might be smart. Sometimes we need things, especially when things break. It seems everything is breaking around here lately, including the very computer I am typing on, so we occasionally need to buy new stuff.

Then we get to the things we want. I have a thing for electronics and guitars. I don't have a large sum invested in these things, but I think about upgrading, or adding to the collection every so often. It's okay to buy stuff. We just need to be wise and thrifty, getting everything we can out of something before replacing it with something new and better.

It's fine to appreciate our worldly possessions along with whatever degree of financial stability we have.

I have noticed with some of my wealthier friends, and even myself, that possessions can take over your life. If you own it, you will need to repair it, maintain it, insure it, and eventually sell it or give it away, and maybe replace it, to start the cycle all over again.

Stuff is a pain. Simplicity is beautiful. Sometimes I wonder why my bookshelves are full of books that I will never refer to again, why my closet is full of clothes I don't wear and why my basement is just full of stuff nobody uses. I love cleaning this stuff out, because it actually improves the quality of my life. I have more space and I can find the things I am looking for more easily. Downsizing, or as a friend calls it, "purging" can bless someone else and cause us to begin to seriously think about how little we really need.

There is something very healthy, although counterintuitive, and almost un-American about giving funds and possessions away. For former churchgoers, we need to break through the wall of guilt that caused us to give large sums of money only to the local church and Christian organizations. That's a fine thing to do if that's where your heart is.

For years after pulling out of church, I looked for a Christian ministry or two to regularly support. I found one in this country that was a wonderful grace-based teaching ministry and another one that helped African leaders battle easily curable diseases by working with them to drill wells so they could have clean drinking water. We have also given one-time gifts to local arts institutions that we frequent.

Lately, we have been more focused on getting our own financial house in order. Several times a year I need to travel to Missouri to help my family there. That is a basic financial responsibility to me. That is giving. I feel like I should be supporting Wisconsin Public Radio because I benefit so much from their morning programming. I will probably eventually do that.

I function through sensing purpose, I look for the giving opportunities that are the closest to me, the closest to my heart and a part of my world.

The point is, this thing is wide open. Give cheerfully, meaningfully, and in a way that causes people to be thankful to God. It might be helping out a family member, a neighbor, a homeless person or someone on the other side of the world. Give to someone or some cause close to your heart.

Of course, giving is not just about money. It's about time and our abilities too. Those things are often more difficult to give because time is currency and most of us value it very highly. Making a donation is quick and easy, but the deeper our involvement and the greater our sacrifice; the more meaningful the act is for everyone.

There is a part of giving that's fun, and there is a part of it that's difficult. Yet if we can give our money and possessions to others in a meaningful way, we experience a new level of freedom. We are not shackled to our wealth and our stuff and we can use them to be a blessing to someone else. Knowing that our gift helped someone else and made them thankful to God is the icing on the cake.

Discoveries:

Remembering Old Lessons that Seem New Again

Here's what I don't get. Why are the most important lessons in life the ones we never master? Why do we have to keep relearning them? Why are we always in one of life's remedial classes, learning about something that we thought we had mastered decades ago?

We know these things. We can recite the correct answers. But when we need that lesson in the course of life, when the pressure is on, we frequently respond with some stupid, knee-jerk reaction, as though the particular life lesson were something we'd never heard of. This must be why the Apostle Paul was so fond of saying, "I put you in remembrance of…"

We can explain an ill-advised reaction as being more emotional than knowledge driven. But knowledge also fails us, because reactions to the stuff that life brings our way come from some place deeper. Our emotions often mislead us and our vast hours of learning may also fail us. These things are a matter of the will, and are based on a lifetime of experience and our most tenaciously held values.

This section of the book is devoted to lessons that I have not mastered and still fail to heed more often than I would like to admit. They are tidbits of truth that have popped up and keep popping up over the last several years as I have tried to take a fresh look at what I believe and how I want to live. They are gradually becoming more of a normal part of who I am. One thing is for sure; life works better when I remember these things.

eight

Making Peace with Yourself

Conditional Grace

Grace is the most counter-intuitive, mysterious thing in the world. It doesn't make any sense at all.

Christians seem to be particularly confused and conflicted about grace. They sing about it, preach about it, and would fight other Christians who disagreed with them about it.

They say grace refers to God's unmerited favor, his giving us the opposite of what we deserve. It's <u>G</u>od's <u>R</u>iches <u>A</u>t <u>C</u>hrist's <u>E</u>xpense. They make it very clear that our redemption and acceptance by God is based entirely on his grace and not our attempts at good works. We declare we cannot be good enough for him to accept us, because "all of our righteousnesses are as filthy rags." (Isaiah 64:6)

They champion grace as the basis for beginning our relationship with God, but go on to uphold a "Christian life" built by works, practices, and adhering to a prescribed system of expectations, i. e., the antithesis of grace.

They say, "You are saved by grace," but you quickly learn that certain behaviors and lifestyles will not be tolerated. There are particular things you must believe in order to be well grounded, and you must even use the correct terminology. You must be supportive of the church program with your finances and volunteer service to be considered mature.

This mindset harbors a conditional acceptance that stands in complete contrast to God's unconditional acceptance. In other words, "God accepts you as you are, but now you're going to have to prove yourself to us. Here's the pattern. This is what a good Christian believes and does." It's a one-pathway-fits-all program.

The church likes to draw lines. You're in or you're out. You're right or you're wrong. You're saved or you're lost; something determined by outward acts like praying a prayer, saying the right words, or being baptized. If you meet the requirements, you can be a church member; otherwise you're not part of the "in group."

Their acceptance depends on which side of the line you are on. There is little room for mystery or individuality.

There are so many things I have heard preached against in my life, that it's laughable. Most are no longer Christian taboos and seem silly now that the culture is at a much different place. Some are still are taboo in some Christian circles.

Men with long hair
Women with short hair
Women wearing slacks
Women wearing short skirts
Women working outside the home
Smoking
Drinking
Gambling
Living together outside of marriage
Being gay

There was a long period in Evangelicalism when we were thought to hate gays and women who had abortions. We truly are better known for what we are against than for what we are for.

We can argue the rightness or wrongness of abortion and homosexuality. However, I understand my response to people is to love, not passing judgment on them or trying to determine who is in and who is out. The problem is coming off as hateful toward huge segments of humanity who didn't have a Christian American postcard kind of life.

Grace has not penetrated the heart of the church.

I wish I could say I have not been guilty of any of the graceless ways of the church. It's funny how we go along with the group and ignore that voice from within that tells us, "This just doesn't seem right."

Honestly, when it comes to grasping grace, I am an even bigger obstacle than the church. It is much easier for me to embrace the tenets of grace for other people than for myself.

I have a tendency to rehash the negative things about me over and over, again and again. I want to get those things fixed. I feel shame because of them. I accept others with their issues, but sometimes I can't stand myself. I am indeed my own worst enemy.

I remember reading how Brennan Manning, author of *The Ragamuffin Gospel*, and many other books written to help us grasp God's grace, loathed himself because of his relapses into alcoholism. Grace is easy to preach, hard to extend to others, and monumentally difficult to accept for ourselves. That's because we know the dirt on ourselves better than anyone. We know it all! We not only know our past but we know we keep doing some of those things, things that disgust us.

If we don't grasp grace in a very personal sort of way, we are never free. There is something constantly hanging over us. It makes it hard to be fully present in the moment. It makes it hard to fully engage another person. It makes it hard to live out the life God wants for us. For too many of us our default mental preoccupation is self-loathing. We worry about our past, our future, and how people must see us. There is always a dark cloud hanging over our heads.

Counter-intuitive Christ

Enter Jesus! He really messed things up!

God becoming a baby born to an unmarried teenager is an interesting concept. God loving all of the wrong people... prostitutes, greedy cheaters, traitors, rough and angry blue collar types, beggars, deformed people, individuals with disgusting diseases, terrorists, and enemy soldiers is also very counter-intuitive. He deliberately reached out to people that his society had completely written off. They were the outcasts, the untouchables. He touched them, healed them, told them stories and went to their parties.

He made enemies of all the wrong people...people in authority who could have him killed, religious and political aristocrats, legalists, the vaunted priestly class, politicians, and the powerful. Sometimes he was very harsh with them.

But he exuded grace when he welcomed children, afforded new status to women, and told engaging stories to large groups of people that followed him. The way he engaged the outcasts and common people was a very new thing! He not only accepted them as they were, but he made it a priority to connect with them.

Most Christians would be quick to point to his death on the cross as evidence of his grace. That's great. Just don't leapfrog over his life to get there.

Several biblical passages make a connection between Christ's death on the cross and our status with God, our life on earth and beyond. Words like redemption, sacrifice, and reconciliation are used to describe the meaning of Christ's death for us.

In the Old Testament people brought animal sacrifices to God. Throughout history people have done all sorts of crazy things, from human sacrifice to self-torture and deprivation to trying to keep impossible rules to appease God. Then he brought all of the dying and the trying to an end.

In Christ, God says, "Enough! No more killing! No more trying to be good enough! There is nothing more to be done. I sent my son to show you how to live, he died because of that. You're redeemed, reconciled. I accept you as you are. Stop trying to earn my favor. Now show the world who I am."

Instead, he asks us to be living sacrifices to represent him in a manner like that of Jesus to the people in our world. A good deal of the time we drop the ball, but that's our mission. That's why we are here. Our life is a response to his love and grace, not a condition for it!

Grace Life

I had a pastor friend whose church (Grace Church) merged with another church (New Life Church). They called the new congregation Grace Life Church. I like that.

What does grace life look like?

If I took this grace thing seriously, I would be at peace with myself. I would know that I am totally loved, accepted, and forgiven, and that nothing I could do would ever change that! That brings me the freedom to be focused on other things, like whatever God has put in my heart to be and do, like fully engaging with a person, like smiling and laughing.

It means no guilt, no shame, and no fear, no rehearsing my greatest hits of personal failures. It means I absorb these facts about grace until I believe them all of the time. It means putting down those accusatory feelings as soon as they crop up.

That's part of the story. The other part is to extend the same grace to others as has been extended to us. That means loving people as they are, instead of looking down on them or trying to turn them into projects to be fixed. How about treating people with dignity and giving them the benefit of the doubt? How about being friends with people whose lifestyle takes us out of our comfort zone? How about making friends with people who are supposed to be the enemy?

The grace life is a good life and a good way to live out our faith by counteracting some of the graceless things Christians have said and done; counteracting it with a surprisingly accepting and loving way of relating to people.

nine

The Best Cocktail Ever

Boxes

Modern life is lived in boxes. We live in a box called a home. We get into boxes with wheels on them to go to boxes where we work, called cubicles.

If we go to church it's another box. When you're in, you're in, and when you're out, you know you're out. This box has a reassuring, sturdy feel about it.

That's exactly why so many people like it. It offers them a respite from the other boxes. It is place to have your beliefs affirmed so you can withstand the doubts, questions, and ridicule you might encounter in the rest of life.

The church box is special. It's sacred; everything else is secular.

I remember hearing Bill Hybels say, "The church is the most important thing in the world." It is sacred, holy, set apart, God's means for carrying out his mission on earth. It is the community of people on mission for him.

I certainly regarded it as such. Being a religious professional (a pastor) it came naturally for me. I structured my life so that my church and religious activities were the top priority. Family life, relationships outside of church and the regular necessities of life were all secondary to my religious responsibilities.

I feel like a jerk as I write these words, and I probably was a jerk. Not unlike the young drummer in the movie, *Whiplash* who terminated his relationship with his girlfriend and became an arrogant jerk to his family so he could become one of the greats, someone whose life really mattered.

It all fit me like a glove. It fed my ego. It made my life simpler. I reasoned that I was forfeiting doing lesser things because I was doing something of crucial importance.

Preaching, teaching, studying the Bible, counseling, leading groups, building a church leadership team; those were the truly important things to me. But as I was trying to make God known to people and make the Gospel understandable, I ignored the wonderful natural opportunities in my everyday life. I was fixated on what I deemed to be the sacred, spiritual things.

But what if the ordinary times, the ordinary people, and the ordinary tasks of life are sacred?

Cocktails

Dividing life into secular and sacred; how did we ever come up with that heresy?

Sacred refers to the separate, the holy, something dedicated to a deity or religion. Secular refers to the common or worldly things.

If there is anything true about the way of Jesus, it is that he lived out his faith in regular, everyday life. It was not just something reserved for a special place or a special time. After all, his disciples lived with him and traveled with him. Most of that time probably seemed like anything but religious. They traveled the countryside on foot at the mercy of others' hospitality when it came to having a place to sleep and food to eat. They fought among themselves and much of the time they just didn't get what Jesus was really talking about. It sounds pretty real to me.

People need Jesus in their everyday life. It's insane to segregate them into the sacred and secular, though that is exactly what we have done.

His way is not a special subculture, though we have built a Christian subculture with our Christian schools, Christian music, Christian books, Christian movies, and Christian celebrities. The goal is to expand the sacred and religious sphere so as to insulate us from the secular (dangerous) culture of the real world, effectively creating our own little world. However, the sacred is not always so sacred, especially once it becomes big business. But the secular is also sacred because God is omnipotent and omnipresent. He can't be partitioned out.

Jesus did not get corrupted by living in the real world; the real world got infected by Jesus. The way of Jesus only makes a difference if people leave the Christian ghetto and live real life with real people outside the ghetto in the real world. Rather than trying to separate ourselves from the culture of the world, we need to immerse ourselves in it. As we do, we will find out that Jesus is already there.

Many Christians not only believe in living separate from the world, but also from each other. This form of separation has been the big deal for me all along. It never made much sense.

Southern Baptists are suspicious of the even stricter fundamentalists and vice versa. They each believe the other has got some important points of doctrine wrong. I was a Southern Baptist who went to an independent, fundamentalist college. Everyone looked a little cross-eyed at me. That is an indicator of the suspicion, divisions and arrogance between two religious sects that were close cousins in the grand scheme of the family tree of Christendom.

There was a long list of things that I experienced in my life that didn't seem quite right, but I ignored them for decades. Instead, I thought there must be something wrong with me because these beliefs and practices were such an accepted part of the status quo religion and 0f religious.

I was part of a denomination that expected their churches not to have anything to do with those churches that <u>weren't</u> a part of their little group.

Sadly, The Church had grown to be so in love with itself that if someone walked in from the outside, it wouldn't make sense or even seem welcoming. Eventually, I said "Enough" and discontinued our association with that denomination. Some people thought this was heresy. I became infatuated with the seeker church movement and we made the uninitiated our focus as a church. I did battle with people who hated this, who believed church was only for Christians. I guess that means screw everyone else.

Eventually, I was sort of squeezed out of the church. I'd gotten to where I no longer derived a sense of fulfillment or personal meaning from it. The Sunday experience became frustrating and agitating and I could no longer take the self-focus and arrogance.

But I didn't stop noticing that God was at work. Actually, I noticed it more than ever. Seeing him in so-called secular art, music, and a wide spectrum of humanity was absolutely thrilling. My God had gotten so much bigger. He was not boxed in by the church.

Blended

What does it look like when you chisel away all the centuries of extraneous stuff and it's just you and Jesus in real life? If you jettison the hierarchy, the cathedrals, the massive church campuses, the official clergy, the budgets, the billions of dollars, the stereotypes, the expectations, the power and the politics, what's left?

How real is our faith? If all of the crutches were knocked away, what would we do? What if it were illegal to assemble, the church buildings were closed, and the pastors imprisoned; how would we live out our faith if were just up to us?

With all the outsourcing options gone, would a sense of personal responsibility kick in? Could we keep our faith as a rather normal part of daily life? Would there be enough real spiritual vigor to naturally, and sometimes radically, live out a Jesus energized life that would inspire others?

Some Christian leaders think such conditions as I describe would be horrible and spell the end for the church. I think they would give birth to something a lot more real and more like Jesus.

Every time a new study comes out indicating the rapid rate at which Americans are turning from religion, the aforementioned folks shake their fists at the inclusive, secular culture they believe is destroying the church and threatening the very existence of western civilization.

Some of the hipper Christian leaders, who accept the reality of the changing demographics of belief among Americans, explain how we must reach out to the younger generations and make our church more attractive to them. But most of the reactions to these supposedly alarming trends seem to be geared toward growing, maintaining and protecting an institution that needs a much deeper evaluation.

Since I devoted a whole section to shifts the church needs to make in my last book, *An Irreligious Faith,* I will stay focused on our individual perspective here.

For me, the whole faith-life thing is one big experiment in living. I don't have it all figured out, but I do have a pretty decent handle on what it isn't.

If I have to use special terminology to discuss my faith, it's not real; it's an intellectual exercise. Shoptalk terminology only alienates people further. How can it be real, if we cannot articulate our faith in a way that is understandable to the uninitiated?

Why do we have to keep pulling ourselves out of regular life to continually be further indoctrinated and pumped up? If it is real, we will assume responsibility for our own faith expression and it will be part of how we live every day.

If it takes a whole bunch of special stuff (dedicated buildings, trained professionals, endless programs) to keep us going, then how is that real? If it is real, we will do just fine without that stuff.

If we keep ourselves as isolated in a subculture (Christian schools, Christian music, Christian friends) as much as possible, then how is that real? If it is real, we will be immersed in culture.

That's the easy part.

What does the experiment look like when faith and life are joined at the hip? I can only answer from my personal experience.

I understand a vital, real life faith to be expressed naturally and normally.

It's about letting God out of the box and seeing him at work wherever he is and in whomever he chooses. I used to think that all that happened pretty much within the church.

It's about seeing opportunities to express Jesus-like love wherever they arise. I used to look to church programs for that.

It's about making peace with yourself. We need to accept his grace for ourselves, and learn to be ourselves, rather than trying to live up to expectations. I guess I have spent most of my life being very concerned about the expectations of others and finding it easier extending grace than receiving it.

It's about figuring this stuff out for yourself, rather than relying on someone else to do it for you. Most Christians outsource their spiritual expression to the church.

I think I just segued into the next chapter.

ten

Don't Wait on the Lord

Responsibility

"You need to be responsible, young lady (or man)!" We have all heard words like this and we likely had a similar response.

We realized we were being talked down to. Our exhorter is usually older and deems himself to be much wiser. Likely, he is a bit arrogant and unwilling to enter into our world to find out what is really happening with us. They are forcing some type of expectation on us.

Or maybe, we really deserved it!

A good deal of the time, exhortations to be responsible are ill conceived and annoying, if not personally demoralizing.

Maybe when someone thinks we are being irresponsible, we really are blowing it and should think about our life in a more long-term manner, considering how our decisions affect others. On the other hand, maybe we are being responsible and it just looks different for us and does not necessarily meet someone else's expectations.

Better to be true to yourself and who God made you to be than focusing on who someone else wants you to be. Within that greater purpose, you will have some dues to pay to get where you want to be, but it is a worthy path. We have a responsibility to be true to ourselves but to pursue that goal in the light of our other responsibilities.

The problem with most of us is that we allow our daily responsibilities to totally distract us from our greater responsibility.

Waiting on the Lord

God gets blamed for more stuff that anyone I know. People have claimed that God told them all manner of things, from committing murder, to all out international war, to making just plain stupid and hurtful decisions.

Sometimes God gets credit for things he didn't do. I have heard pastors brag about their churches, how God is doing something special or how the church is growing so fast. Sometimes it's just a subtle way of bragging; a thinly veiled attempt to incite a little jealousy among their colleagues.

Furthermore, what they indicate as God's blessing is usually attributable to something very human. For instance, churches grow when they are in growing areas; that's why inner city churches move to the more affluent suburbs. Churches grow when led by charismatic leaders, though sometimes they are not very nice people. Churches grow when they offer programs that people like, such as spectacular Sunday morning productions. That is part of the attraction of the mega churches. They grow while little churches that can't front an extravagant production or a smorgasbord of programs are unable to keep their doors open. So much of what is called "God's blessing" is directly attributable to leadership and sociological factors.

Do supernatural things happen? Do unexplainable blessings occur? I certainly believe so, but the key factor is the word, "unexplainable."

There is another way that people slander God. It's not in falsely attributing things to him, but in making an excuse to take a totally passive approach to life. It has a name: "waiting on the Lord."

In all fairness, when someone claims they are waiting on the Lord, it can mean things other than opting out of personal responsibility. It may mean, "I don't know what to do, so rather than just doing something that's ill advised, I am waiting until I have more clarity."

But "waiting on the Lord" can become a convenient excuse. It can be a pseudo spiritual way of saying "I am just going to keep my nose down and do what is expected of me," rather than get in touch with the still small voice within me and find out what I really should be pursuing.

Or maybe it really means, "I am waiting for some sort of sign to help me to decide," rather than, carefully considering the issue and making an informed decision.

I used to think like that. If a door opened, it was God. If it didn't, I was waiting on the Lord.

For some people, "waiting on the Lord" simply means, "I'm stuck." I have felt like that at several different junctures in my life. While I think we need to get a little more comfortable with living through a difficult process and not having everything figured out, everyone needs some direction and sense of purpose.

To get unstuck you need to get moving. The problem is that some of us are such sticklers for making sure we do the right thing, that we do nothing. Some of us are so fearful and risk adverse that we don't try. We are too afraid of making mistakes.

We never have things figured out very well ahead of time; we have to try things and learn as we are doing. Then we have to tweak things again and again.

Sometimes by getting moving we learn we are moving in the wrong direction, but the process gives us greater clarity about the path we should be on. Making mistakes can be a huge positive in life.

We let fear paralyze us. We can say we are waiting on the Lord, when he is waiting on us.

Freedom

"Responsibility" is a heavy-sounding word, but assuming personal responsibility is about freedom (a lighter-sounding word). When you have freedom, you get responsibility. If no one is mandating what to do, you need to figure it out for yourself. You need to be responsible with your freedom.

You don't have to meet anyone's expectations; you're free from that! You are not hostage to anyone else unless you choose to serve someone out of love.

You don't have to do what is expected, so you are not bound by expectations that people try to force on you. You're free.

You don't serve a capricious God who leads by spectacular, mystical signs. You know a loving God speaks through that internal voice you keep hearing but have too often ignored. Actually, he speaks in a multitude of ways that can involve relationships and circumstances, as well as inner promptings.

The point is your spiritual expression is yours. You no longer look for an easy way to outsource it, making yourself subservient to a spiritual private contractor. How you express your faith is up to you. A whole new world just opened up.

That's the freedom part. But the freedom creates a vacuum called responsibility.

You get to set your own personal values, goals, and objectives. You get to find out who you really are. You may have put that off for a long time. Some people never get around to it.

You are no longer frozen into status quo inactivity. You get to dream, imagine, and take steps in the direction of your true identity.

You realize God speaks to your heart and you learn to hear and trust him.

Then how you express your faith is your decision. You get to figure these things out for yourself.

How will YOU worship God? How will YOU serve others? How will YOU live a more sustainable life? How will YOU experience community and relationships?

I believe that God has left way more in our court than I ever thought. We are not his drones. He doesn't do cookie cutter anything. He relates to us individually. He is not trying to make us something we are not, but is trying to get us to release the potential he put within us.

There is so much power in our personal story, our personal identity and our unique passions and abilities that when we act in accordance with who we really are it may scare some people.

So, go scare somebody.

eleven

Can You Hear Me Now?

Preoccupied Pastor

I am absent minded. I lose track of my eyeglasses and my coffee every day. When I get ready to go somewhere, I often return to the house from the garage to pick up something I should have taken with me. Behind the wheel, if I am in conversation or deep thought, the odds of me missing a turn are roughly 50 /50.

My mind is out in front of my reality. It is playing advance man, while AWOL from the present.

My family and a few close friends are painfully aware of my absent-mindedness. I have always been this way. My fear is that someday I might have Alzheimer's or dementia of some other variety and no one will notice. That's the family joke. "Your Dad is out wandering in the street. Oh, he has always done that."

What is preoccupying my mind to such a degree that I have lost touch with the present?

Usually, I am thinking about the future or the past. That's what people worry about; things that have happened, that they can't change, and things that can't be dealt with because they are in the future and likely, will never happen.

My obsessive-compulsive tendencies and Christianity has made for a preoccupied life.

My behavior and mental processes were fueled by expectations; expectations others had of me, expectations I had of others and, worst of all, expectations I had of myself.

All of those expectations were, at least, doubled because I was a pastor. That's why pastors flame out, drop out, and opt out. The immense weight and wide array of expectations thrust upon them, along with the ones their hyper-responsible personality generates, are simply too much.

The sheer weight of my responsibilities, coupled with an excessive sense of personal responsibility, a belief that church work was the most important thing in the world, and the need to be needed, led me to literally ignore my neighbor while on my way to a church meeting. I was the Levite in the story of The Good Samaritan, too busy with my religious duties to help someone in need.

Here is a sample of my self-talk. (Everybody talks to themselves.)

Future-oriented self-talk:
"Let's see, what's next?"
"Are you sure that's the best order to do things?"
"How will I do it?"
"What will I say?"
"What will they think of me?"
"I hope this isn't another flop or disappointment."

Past-oriented self-talk:
"Why doesn't he like me?"
"Why hasn't he contacted me?"
"Did I do something wrong?"
"I can't believe I did that! I'm so ashamed!"
"I need to review (again and again) all the decisions that got me here, to see if I did something wrong."

This is the kind of mental spin cycle that kept me from being completely present in the moment. But I am happy to report that I'm doing much better now.

Traumatic Transition

I'm not there yet, but I have mellowed out tremendously. I wonder why?

Well, I couldn't have been wound much tighter.

Mostly I mellowed out because I had no choice. Things happened; unexpected, unwanted things.

Different kinds of people came into my life that I hadn't had to deal with before and I had to learn to accept them and love them.

My dreams got dashed again and again.

People disappointed me so many times that I become cynical.

We all get some hard miles on our odometer of life.

If my own personality and my life-consuming vocation weren't enough, I had these surprises to deal with.

It was painfully difficult for me to come down from the high I received from being the go to guy as a pastor, to being a regular Joe. It was hard for me to adjust to a phone that didn't ring, when it used to ring all the time. I complained about the incessant intrusions, but make no mistake, I loved it. It proved to me that I was needed, I mattered, I was important.

I felt like I was on a fast moving train that came to a screeching halt and sent everything that wasn't tied down flying, hitting me in the back of the head. I was jittery and angry. Things were yanked out from under me. I didn't know what to do or even who I was. A bunch of unwanted things happened together; the collapse of a church, the death of my two best friends, the loss of my employment and my identity. I was in shock. Hurt. Angry. Lost.

I lost a vocation, and eventually a relationship with the church, that gave me a method to express my faith, my gifts, and my personality. Basically, it involved a service, a class, a group or a program to do anything. Learning how to express my faith without any of that was a whole new ball game for me.

Mr. Mellow

Slowly, I learned I did not need the structure of a church program to do something Jesus-like; I just needed to do it as the opportunities arose.

I can talk to my neighbor and give him my full attention because I am not on the way to a church meeting. Finally, chatting with him is more important than mowing my yard.

I can worship God in nature or in a crowd of people at a secular event, because I am not tied to a 10:30am Sunday event at a church building.

I can be inspired by secular art, music and literature, because it really is all sacred.

As a child of God redeemed by Christ, I really ought to be the happiest, most relaxed, totally present in the moment person on earth.

I have to remind myself of these things all of the time, but it is getting better.

twelve

The Only Life Worth Living

Being Right

Everyone likes winning. But every time someone wins, someone, or several someones, lose. The thrill of winning usually keeps us from thinking about the losers. Victory trumps empathy.

It just feels good being right; having the right answer, being correct, being the most astute, identifying with the right group, being a part of the "true Church," and being the best. Everyone likes to come out on top.

But two things happen to us when we win; we feel great and we think we are better than our competitors.

Too bad we can't confine these feelings to board games. Unfortunately, the desire to be "better than" is pervasive.

Church history is a showcase for the concept. Every council, every split, every denomination has its own brand of being "better than." It has been going on for nearly 2000 years. That's why there are so many sects and denominations.

The result of our being "better than" is arrogance and exclusion. In the context of the Christian faith, these attitudes are nothing short of bizarre.

We have a redeemer and leader who loved the losers and infuriated those who felt they were superior to most of humanity. He lifted the oppressed and pronounced judgment on the oppressors. In old school preacher speak, "He comforted the afflicted and afflicted the comfortable." He was the friend of sinners and a thorn in the side of the so-called righteous "better thans."

There has always been a dissonance in Christendom that has caused people to point the finger of hypocrisy back at the church. The inner conflict rages between truth and love; the desire to be right and the mandate to love.

Christians have defended the faith and pointed out sin, becoming the self-appointed guardians not only of the church but also of "the American way of life." They have pushed a package of values that were a mishmash of biblical teaching, nationalism, tradition, and things that made them feel comfortable.

And they have made no secret about what they are against. Their message was received loud and clear. The church is a place for Norman Rockwell-esque families only.

Their defending the faith offended their founder and the desire to be right led them into error.

They neglected the one thing that is the most important thing, to love God and others. Instead of loving others as they love themselves, they loved themselves so much that they rejected those who were not like them.

I was one of them, and I still have my issues with loving people out of my comfort zone.

Scattergories

Here is a convenient way to decide who is "in" and who is "out", who we will love and who we will hate (or disregard). Stick a label on them.

We have Liberals, Conservatives, Progressives, Calvinists, Hyper-Calvinists, Moderate-Calvinists, Pre-tribulationalists,

Post-tribulationalists, Mid-tribulationalists, Armenians, Fundamentalists, Denominationalists, Methodists, Baptists (Southern, General, Regular, Independent, and Free Will), Catholics, Presbyterians, Anglicans, Lutherans, Christian Church, Church of Christ, Pentecostal, Assemblies of God and Independents (There are scores of labels within most of these categories.) Everyone holds their label of "rightness" as though it were some sort of badge of honor, because they are "right". The attempt to publicize their rightness with the names of various groups is really quite humorous.

A lot of these groups shun the others like the plague, as though they feel they might be corrupted by their theological error.

But wait, there's more! There are the ethnic slurs, and the social economic ones, like "trailer trash" and "welfare queen."

Mexican, Black, Liberal, Progressive, Conservative and Libertarian are all loaded terms in our sensitive times. Their mere mention often brings a stereotype to our minds.

Once you categorize people, you can ignore them. You don't need to think about them anymore, except for the reminder that they are wrong, misguided, devalued, lost. You don't need to get to know anyone from your personal blacklist of groups as individuals, because you already have the whole group pegged.

And so, we have successfully devalued the most important thing in the universe, the most important thing to God: a person.

Our role on earth, as I understand it, is to love God and people, not to categorize and judge them.

Messy

It's tidy to reduce our faith to an intellectual exercise of systematic theology and positions on various topics. You can make a checklist to see if someone is right or wrong. It's tidy to categorize the losers who get it wrong. I'm right, they're wrong! Done.

But love is always messy. That's because it's unconditional. So you learn to love people who are messed up and have real issues. They will disappoint you and try your patience because being messed up is the universal condition of human beings. It's always there when get we past the human hologram that projects how wonderful we are. Loving people will take you places you never wanted to go.

You can't fix them, but you can love them. They will disappoint you. They will not always like you. But then, we disappoint others and are not always likeable either.

Love is the hardest, easiest, most strenuous, natural, frustrating, fulfilling thing we ever do.

There are lots of ways that people try to change other people. A lot of them are manipulative. Some are well meaning. None of them work.

Love works! Love is right, and is the only way of being right that doesn't require someone to be "right" and someone to be "wrong."

Loving people as they are and learning to love ourselves, warts and all, is the most transformative thing a human being can ever do. There is a connection between the two.

Interesting that we have come back to loving ourselves. Love comes from God. He loves us and if we don't get it, we can't give it. It's hard to accept that we are loved by God, really loved, no matter what. It's hard to love ourselves in accordance with the way he loves us.

It's a basic building block of life and is the very core of our faith and our relationship with him. It's the freedom to stop trying to be good enough or right enough. It's the freedom to quit worrying about what we have done. It gets us out from under the cloud of guilt and shame so we can feel his sunshine.

Our response to that love makes us want to love other people the same way even when they are different, even when they are supposed to be the enemy, even when they frustrate us.

thirteen

A Good Mystery

The Fear of Certainty

Ever wonder what is behind the certainty that some Christians claim they have about things that are impossible to verify?

Obviously, it takes faith to be a person of faith. But I am thinking about folks who claim they understand God's position on every point of doctrine and every contemporary issue. I used to think that way myself.

A hunger for mental tidiness drives people to embrace detailed doctrinal positions on matters of faith. There is a natural human desire to have things figured out, to have the pieces of the puzzle fit together nicely to form a beautiful picture of a belief system or systematic theology that answers all of the questions and affirms our presuppositions.

To buy into a system that already has that figured out for you can be both satisfying and convenient. Then, you don't have to do the hard work of figuring out what you believe for yourself. You can simply attach your wagon to someone else's horse and follow them. That is the convenience of embracing creeds, denominational and local church statements of faith, and following religious teachers like mega church pastors.

This helps to explain both the historical popularity and the current decline of all of those institutions of faith. People of a passing era were better at playing follow the leader. They were more trusting of both their leaders and their organizations.

Today, people are more cynical, less trusting, and more likely to vet groups before joining them. That's because there have been so many self-serving and corrupt leaders exposed and because so many of our institutions have reached a point in their history where they are no longer serving the people but the people are serving them.

Today we are witnessing a decline in the popularity of institutions with a top-down leadership approach. In some ways, power really is slowly beginning to return to the people.

Yet there is still a love of certainty. I expect that an obsessive need to have everything figured out has made a lot of people fundamentalists, and atheists.

Fundamentalists cling to an ancient creed, or historical figure in church history they believe best honors the meaning of the biblical text. They tend to think the church's and nation's best days are behind us because we have strayed from the text (the Bible or the Constitution) and they believe all of the answers are there in the text.

Some fundamentalists and other religionists eventually become atheists when they realize they can't reconcile everything in the Bible and make everything they think they know about God fit together as perfectly as they once believed. Their house of cards crumbles.

Being a person of faith and feeling the need to figure everything out really don't fit well together. That's why it is called faith, because you don't have it all figured out.

That doesn't mean that a person of faith is an idiot or simpleton. It just means you come to the conclusion that you don't have God all figured out, and those who seem to have him all figured out really don't either. So you hold on to what you can understand and what you choose to believe, and you don't sweat the rest.

I confess, after forty-one years of marriage I don't have my wife figured out. After sixty-one years of being me I don't even have myself figured out. Why would I even dare to assume I have God figured out?

One more thing about certainty; every once in a while something happens that makes you wonder if you might be off a little here or there. You wonder if maybe you are a little too certain. Maybe your neighbor isn't bound for Hell because he's not a Calvinist.

Once your house of cards starts shaking, you have to do something. Some people become more inclusive, some totally reject the faith, and some just fake a kind of nominal belief without really dealing with these issues.

But the most common response a person has when their belief system begins to feel a little shaky is to defend it against all threats. That helps to explain the centuries of fighting between Christian groups throughout church history over various points of theology. But that's still not the biggest issue with presumed certainty about the details of our faith.

Arrogance is the natural response to thinking you are right, along with the thought that people who differ with you are wrong. Pride is the most insidious aspect of being totally certain about all of the details of religious belief, and the Bible indicates pride to be the root of sin. You can't help but see the irony of the close relationship between religion, so-called doctrinal purity, and pride.

The Comfort of Mystery

I have more questions than ever. Age does that. You become more certain about a few things and less certain about a lot of things.

Both lists that follow are really the shortlists and somewhat random. They could be better organized and much longer.

Some of things I am certain of (or choose to believe) include:

- Life has more unexpected twists and turns than you could ever imagine.
- The hardest times present the best opportunities for change and growth.
- It is best to be who we really are, rather than trying to fake it or meet someone else's expectations.
- We need to find a way to do the things that flow from our heart and make us feel alive.
- Pursuing important things takes more perseverance than we ever thought it would.
- If we understand how God sees us, we will experience wonderful inner peace and a sense of wellbeing.
- Relationships make life worth living. There is nothing more important than people.
- Some people will hurt us, but we can't give up on loving people and building relationships.
- Jesus is God.
- We find our inspiration for how to live life by looking at how Jesus lived life.
- Believing he is who he said he is, is the crux of life.
- He redeemed us from any need to be good enough to gain God's favor.
- We are therefore not condemned because of our sins.
- We are not defined by our sins but by how God sees us and by the wonderful potential he put within us.

Things I don't understand:

- How people can be so cruelly inhuman to their fellow man
- Why logical and good things don't work out

- Why life is so hard and filled with so much pain
- Why God seemed to instigate genocide in the Old Testament
- Why it seems that those who have never heard the good news about Jesus are doomed
- Why some of the instructions to churches in the New Testament seem sexist, overly structured, and generally not very workable for our time
- Why prayers seem to be responded to in a capricious manner
- The end times and the book of Revelation
- Why there is so much contrast between Jesus and his church, and why Christians and church leaders seem to be okay with it
- Why natural disasters happen
- Why bad things happen to good people
- Why children die

The Vanity of Answers

As any student taking a test will tell you, some questions are far more answerable than others. And any teacher will tell you, some answers are better than others. It seems almost any answer we could give to these difficult questions could be followed by a, "Yeah, but what about... ."

For example, people are so cruel to one another because there is no limit to the potential for good or evil in the human soul and God has allowed us to make our own choices (though a Calvinist may disagree).

But what about a Hitler, Stalin, or Sadam Hussein who killed hundreds of thousands? Why didn't God somehow prevent that? Is he that hands-off with humanity? Yet people thank him for getting a job or a good parking place, claiming he is intimately concerned about the minutiae of their lives. Which is it? Is he closely involved, or hands off?

Why don't good things work out and why do bad things happen to good people?

We could say we simply don't understand all of the implications, and God does. In some places in scripture it seems God rewards good behavior. Frequently, the church teaches that good behavior will be rewarded. "If you do this, God will do that." Then why all of the injustice? Why would God allow so much pain to befall his precious creation, even those who follow him?

What about the Old Testament genocide, where it seems that God wants his people to kill everyone in another tribe including men, women, children, and even the animals?

We could respond that they must have been terribly evil and unredeemable people. God had to keep his people from being corrupted by their influence. It was a violent world back then, it was the only way his people could survive.

Maybe God is schizophrenic; because it seems he is quite the opposite in the New Testament. Maybe the people misunderstood God and simply responded in a typical cultural manner to the threat.

What is the connection between geography and salvation? If I were born on most other continents, the likelihood of my being Christian would be very slim. So what's the story for those people who have the misfortune of being born somewhere where Christianity is not prevalent? If God is omnipotent and omnipresent, why isn't he there saving people like he is here?

We could respond that it's why we need missionaries. Or maybe that they are just bad, unredeemable people. Or maybe that God is active there in a different way, below the radar.

I have two conclusions about the whole issue of the mystery of God (and life).

Ask questions, because anything that is true can withstand any question we could ever think of.

I think it is important to explore these topics, but it is also important not to settle for simplistic, trite answers that are not really answers at all. Usually, the best answer to something mysterious is, "I don't know." That's why it is called a mystery.

But mystery messes with our minds, as though we have assembled a beautiful scene from a jigsaw puzzle box, but several key pieces are missing. There is a lot of beauty revealed, but you can't help yourself from getting fixated on the missing pieces. And those pieces are nowhere to be found.

What do we do?

I think we accept what is before us, both the beauty and the mystery. Both are definitely true of God, and life.

fourteen

Hello, World!

Out of the Cage

I wondered for a long time how to summarize one hundred and eighty-two pages into a physical image. I finally got a picture in my mind that the cover artist for my first book, *An Irreligious Faith,* captured beautifully.

On the cover is a birdcage that strangely reminds you of a church, with its tiny stained glass window and cross on top. It is rather elaborate, but it still is a cage. The door of the cage has swung open and in the far distance you can see the silhouette of a person walking into a brighter land, perhaps a city.

First, the cage, then the brighter land.

The cage, representing the institutional church, has serious issues. It's in trouble. People are abandoning it in droves.

Since I wrote about those issues in *An Irreligious Faith,* I will only summarize them here. These are generalizations, which means they are generally correct but there are some wonderful exceptions in local churches here and there.

The church…

- has its own separate culture. Living out our faith in the real world seems more like Jesus.

- is a convenient, but irresponsible way to outsource our spiritual expression. I can't find a legitimate basis for this approach.
- has become self-serving. There is too much emphasis on sustaining and growing the organization and too little effort devoted to serving people as an act of love.
- has become unloving and unaccepting. In an effort to be correct, it has lost its authority by becoming unloving.
- is not a safe place to ask questions. There are too many pat answers and strange looks given in response to good, honest questions.
- suffers from top-down leadership. That discounts the value of an individual and opens the door to possible spiritual abuse and cultishness.
- sucks up resources. There is so much spent on buildings and staff that seems like it would be put to better use on external needs.

When someone parts ways with the institutional church, the first thing they should do is complain. By that, I mean list their grievances as I have done above.

The next thing they should do is grieve. Finding it necessary to leave the institutional church behind is disheartening. It's not what we expected. We are losing our expectations and hopes for the church, for a community, for our own sense of belonging and purpose. Usually, some relationships become casualties in the process of leaving. That is a major loss. We should give ourselves some time to move through the grieving process.

Then, stop complaining and get on with life. Don't get stuck there or you and all of those around will be miserable.

So much for the cage.

Into the Blue

"The blue" has a couple of things going for it.

In the blue you are free from the confines of institutional ways of expressing your faith. You are free from outsourcing your faith expression to an organization. How you deal with that is now up to you.

You are free to explore the unknown of what your free-range faith will look like.

You are free from institutionalism, and free to express your faith in a way that is authentic, meaningful, and refreshing to you.

That will require some creativity.

Scripture proclaims that we are God's work of art. He created us to be artists, not just critics. You may be thinking you don't have an artistic bone in your body. I certainly used to think that way. But being an artist is not a rare gift; it is a common one.

Artists create. I know it seems like life is something out of our control and we are just responding to what happens to us. Yet, even in those reactions, we are creating responses that shape our lives and influence others. Since we share an image and likeness with God, we share a bit of his artistry.

That means we design and create things. Our choices and pursuits design and create the way we live. The way we do even mundane tasks reveals the kind of person we are. But there is some aspect of creativity within each of us that is one of the most significant contributions we can make to the world.

It might be something as practical as the way we relate to people, the way we repair things, an ability to teach others, or the skill to prepare an excellent meal.

It could be more in line with what we normally think of as art, like painting, sculpting, writing, photography, or acting.

We each have our special contribution to make. Don't deny it. Discover it, cultivate it, and use it.

One aspect of creating that I have addressed throughout this book is forging our own, personal ways of spiritual expression.

We are free to do it. We don't have to be tied to expectations or an institution. You cannot use those excuses any longer. We are walking out into the brighter place, into the blue. God is already there, and this new larger realm of God's working is without limit.

We get to figure this out for ourselves. You believe Jesus is who he said he was? As a result, you love him and others and aspire to live in his ways? How are going to do it?

How will you absorb and share his love? How will you live your life to its fullest, being who he created you to be? How will you cultivate loving relationships with him and others?

Repurposed

Here is an article I wrote after a weekend away last winter.

You caught me! I am doing nothing. Well, I am typing. But in general, for the last couple of days, I have done nothing.

It's called a vacation; really a three day mini getaway. We came to a place where there is nothing to do and are staying in a place that has no TV or Internet connection. Our abode, constructed in 1877, has two-foot thick limestone walls, so we hear nothing. It's tomb quiet in here.

We are indeed surrounded by nothingness. Even the landscape is basic winter - bleak, white snow, brown sticks, gray haze. No color, no signs of life. Just rolling hills of lonely nothingness.

Once the body-tremors from media deprivation subsided, I began to love the nothingness. I took in the rustic and whimsical nature of our temporary home. I read, and obviously, I wrote.

This small, southwestern Wisconsin town, born in the lead mine boom days of the late nineteenth and early twentieth centuries, was settled by Cornish immigrants. During the Great Depression of the nineteen-thirties it hit the skids. Fortunately, thoughtful entrepreneurs began restoring these amazing limestone and brick buildings, and gradually various types of artists moved in. Today the community promotes art forms from pottery to writing to the architectural revival of these noble structures.

However, the town feels deserted on this blah February Sunday. Shops are closed. People have headed home after a big community event Saturday. Everyone seems to be hunkered down for the winter.

We have seen some signs of life. Art abounds in our rough-hewn apartment of 138-year-old massive stones and 6×6 beams. I feel like the beams and stones alone could tell some pretty good stories. But when the stonemason turned this place into living quarters just a few years ago, he imbedded bits of fossils, glass, spikes, marbles, and little fish in the bathroom wall. The décor includes an old theater seat, a commercial weighing scale, and beat up old trunks. It's weird, but beautiful.

We found an amazing pottery shop that was actually open on this forsaken day. It was built as a brewery in 1878. Now, the potters live upstairs, loving their life in this artists' community, adoring the huge old stone brewery repurposed as their studio, gallery, and home. Practical me thought the place to be a maintenance nightmare. Yet, I love artists putting it all on the line, fighting for survival while living out their dream.

There is a town just a few miles from here with lots of shops. It's a serious tourist attraction for the state of Illinois, just across the state line. There, we patronized a young man's coffee shop and bakery on his second day of operation. He was nervous and apologetic that everything wasn't perfect. We had fun affirming him and his dream.

A few art galleries also impressed and inspired. So it wasn't all nothingness.

Everywhere we went, we encountered repurposed materials turned into art. Just about every piece of furniture, décor, and building material in our little home from yesteryear was old, old, old.

The brewery became a pottery studio. The old storefront became a young man's brand new business venture. Old car parts and things I would consider worthless crap were fashioned into art.

In the midst of old discarded stuff, people are dreaming and creating. In the process, they honor the weathered, rusty uniqueness of each piece, while turning it into a beautiful new creation.

Then there is me. Old, dinged-up, hoping for new purpose and adventure.

A little too sappy? Too self-revelatory? Too vulnerable and honest?

Well, maybe this is about me, or maybe, it is about you.

Or us. I wonder.

Here's to a life, in which wonder never ceases, art keeps on being fashioned, and new purpose is continually being discovered.

Amen!

Conclusion

A lot of people are going to tell you that you're nuts for trying to live out a life of faith away from the church and religious institutions. A lot of people are wrong.

Churches, like people, come in all shapes and sizes. Some are so in love with their traditions and so out of touch with the real world, that they are irrelevant. Thankfully, some are beginning to take the initiative to tangibly represent the Gospel and love of God to their neighbors. Some are self-serving; others are trying to bless people in their communities.

Most churches are some combination of these positive and negative traits, just like individuals.

A faith apart from its institutional elements is not for everyone, so there is no need to try to force it. You will know if it fits you, or not.

But the trend is away from the institution and toward something more personal, more relational, and more authentic. And those are great values.

That has left a lot of people flailing in some sort of vacuum trying to figure things out.

They may wonder:

Am I a heretic?

Why did my church friends desert me?

Are there other people like me?

How can I cultivate my faith, but still keep it real?

Those are the questions I have tried to address in this and my previous book.

You are not a heretic because you have issues with cultural Christendom.

After using most of these pages to describe the validity of a free range faith, I feel I must list the dangers like those disclaimers in television commercials for prescription drugs.

If you have been a part of the church, the transition to a free-range faith will take a while and it will have some challenges. Those may include some strained relationships with your church-going friends, but you will find new friends, and new interests to fill the vacuum.

You may feel alone, but you are in a company of millions of people.

You may wonder if you are a heretic as you are drawn to re-evaluate your beliefs, but you will find a more authentic faith in the process.

When I hear the words, "free range," I immediately think of chickens and the way they were raised back in the days of the family farm. These yard birds had a place to shelter from the weather and food to eat when it could not be found through their own foraging. Yet they were free to roam. They made their own choices.

We have come a long way since those days; feeding chickens growth hormones, freakishly accelerating their development, getting them plump in a hurry. They are squeezed into metal buildings with no space and nothing to do but eat, grow fat and be slaughtered. Every chicken is contained in its tiny space for life, until sacrificed for the "greater good." The chickens are all treated the same and they all do pretty much the same thing because they think they have no choice.

They probably don't know they can make their own decisions and they probably don't know they can fly.

Should one escape the containment facility, it will need to adjust to living in the real world. If the chicken could speak to us (or if we could understand chicken speak), I think it would say, "There is nothing better than being free, but it's really different, and I had to adjust to it. But there is no way I am going back!"

Notes

Introduction

1. Jack Wellman, "The Decline of the American Church," *Christian Crier* (website), (November 24, 2015 8:50PM), http://www.patheos.com/blogs/christian-crier/2013/10/26/why-we-are-losing-so-many-churches-in-the-united-states, October 26, 2013

2. Warren Bird, "More than 100 Million Unchurched in the United States?" *Leadership Network* (website), (November 24, 2015 8:50PM), http://leadnet.org/more_than_100_million_unchurched_in_the_united_states, October 19, 2012

3. "Five Trends Among the Unchurched," *Barna Group* (website), (November 24, 2015 8:50PM), https://www.barna.org/barna-update/culture/685-five-trends-among-the-unchurched#.VS02N1xOxSV

All Bible References

Holy Bible, New Living Translation (Wheaton, IL: Tyndale House Publishers, Inc., 1996)

Contact Glenn

Glenn Hager is also the author of *An Irreligious Faith: How to Starve Religion and Feed Life,* available in paperback and ebook editions on Amazon.

His writings can be found at glennhager.com.

You can contact Glenn at glennhager1@gmail.com